CHICKEN!

GOOD HOUSEKEEPING

CHICKEN!

75+ EASY & DELICIOUS RECIPES

★ GOOD FOOD GUARANTEED ★

HEARST
books

HEARSTBOOKS

An Imprint of Sterling Publishing Co., Inc.
1166 Avenue of the Americas
New York, NY 10036

ISBN 978-1-61837-310-6

The Good Housekeeping Cookbook Seal guarantees that the recipes in this publication meet the strict standards
of the Good Housekeeping Institute. The Institute has been a source of reliable information and a consumer
advocate since 1900 and established its seal of approval in 1909. Every recipe in this publication has been
tested until perfect for ease, reliability, and great taste by the Good Housekeeping Test Kitchen.

Hearst Magazine Media, Inc. has made every effort to ensure that all information in this publication is accurate.
However, due to differing conditions, tools, and individual skills, Hearst Magazine Media, Inc.
cannot be responsible for any injuries, losses, and/or damages that may result from
the use of any information in this publication.

Distributed in Canada by Sterling Publishing Co., Inc.
c/o Canadian Manda Group, 664 Annette Street
Toronto, Ontario M6S 2C8, Canada
Distributed in Australia by NewSouth Books
University of New South Wales, Sydney, NSW 2052, Australia

For information about custom editions, special sales, and premium and corporate purchases, please contact
Sterling Special Sales at 800-805-5489 or specialsales@sterlingpublishing.com.

Manufactured in China

2 4 6 8 10 9 7 5 3 1

sterlingpublishing.com
goodhousekeeping.com

Cover and interior design by Scott Russo
Photography credits on page 126

Contents

FOREWORD **7**

INTRODUCTION **9**

Weeknight Favorites 15

Bone-in Chicken 59

Cook It Whole 87

Wings & Ground Chicken 99

Rotisserie Chicken Meals 111

INDEX **124**

PHOTOGRAPHY CREDITS **126**

METRIC CONVERSION CHARTS **127**

CRUNCHY DEVILED CHICKEN
(PAGE 67)

Foreword

How often do you cook chicken? If you're like the majority of Americans it's between two and three times a week. Last year we ate more than 93 pounds of chicken per person, and the number is on the rise! So, we're guessing you're on the hunt for new ideas. In this book we offer more than 75 recipes for roasting, poaching, stir-frying, soup-making, and more. Want to use your Instant Pot, sheet pan, skillet? We've got you covered.

When plotting the book, we talked about how we decide what's for dinner. Sometimes it's a look in the fridge, sometimes a quick trip down the meat aisle on the way home from work. Depending on time (and what you can think of) you'll choose boneless, on-the-bone parts, whole, ground, or a rotisserie. So, we organized our chapters to make it easier than ever to find a favorite for what you have!

Weeknight Favorites (our longest chapter) highlights super-quick prep times for boneless breasts and thighs. Paprika Chicken with Tomatoes (page 45) is a simple one-dish crowd-pleaser and Pancetta Chicken (page 18) is also a sheet pan favorite. Saucy skillet stir-fries from Fiery Kung Pao Chicken (page 25) to Sesame Chicken Stir-Fry (page 27) come together quickly (make sure to complete your prep first). You'll also find chowder, curry, kebabs, sliders, marsala, and more.

Bone-in Chicken features those staple cuts that always seem to be on special sale, so whip up Quick Chicken Mole (page 66), fry Nashville Hot Chicken (page 64), roast Spicy Jerk Drumsticks (page 73), or use your Instant Pot for delicious Quicker Coq au Vin Blanc (page 71).

Cook It Whole boasts roasts like Apple & Thyme Roast Chicken (page 92), Roast Chicken with 40 Cloves of Garlic (page 93), and Lemony Herb Roast Chicken (page 96) as well as a slow cooker favorite Crock-Star Chicken with Walnut Herb Sauce (page 97).

Wings & Ground Chicken provides 5 delicious variations on everyone's favorite game day snack: wings! There's also a yummy Lemon-Dill Chicken Meatball Soup (page 109) that features mini-meatballs, and delicious riffs on meatloaf Plus Thai Basil Stir-Fry (page 105) that competes with your local takeout's Larb dish.

Rotisserie Chicken Meals offer ease for those days when you just don't have time to start from scratch, but want homemade quality meals. We offer a craveable Buffalo Chicken Baguette Pizza (page 112), cheesy Enchiladas Verdes (page 116), a Rotisserrie Chicken Cobb (page 119), and a variety of chicken salads (page 117) from Pesto Chicken Salad Croissants to Curried Grape and Chicken, and Basil & Sundried Tomato.

As you can see, chicken is not just America's favorite meat (yes it has surpassed beef and pork consumption!) it's enjoyed around the world. We hope you'll dig in to this new collection and find new recipes to love. Welcome to your new chicken repertoire!

The editors of *Good Housekeeping*

CROCK-STAR CHICKEN WITH
WALNUT-HERB SAUCE
(PAGE 97)

Introduction

Like many cooks, you're probably serving poultry a couple of times a week—and looking for new inspiration. You're not alone. Last year Americans consumed over 108 pounds of poultry per person. So, like you, we're always on the hunt for new ideas. Luckily, poultry is not just an American favorite; it has found its way into pots around the globe, and flavorful preparations abound. Whether you want to do fix-it-and-forget-it Slow-Cooker Tex-Mex Soup (page 61), a stir-fry like Sesame Chicken Stir-Fry (page 27), or a last-minute skillet like Chicken Marsala Lite (page 37), we have the recipes. And many of them take less than an hour in all.

KNOW YOUR CHICKEN

BROILER-FRYERS Tender young birds that weigh 2½ to 5 pounds. They can be roasted, fried, sautéed, grilled, or broiled.

ROASTERS Meaty birds that usually weigh 6 to 8 pounds and are best when roasted.

CORNISH HENS Small birds that weigh up to 2 pounds each. They are tasty grilled, broiled, or roasted.

FOWL Also called stewing hens, these tough older birds weigh 4 to 6 pounds and are most often available around the holidays. They are best braised or stewed and make the tastiest chicken broth.

CAPONS These are the big boys! Neutered male chickens that weigh 8 to 10 pounds on average. They are very meaty and tender and are usually roasted.

POULTRY SHOPPING CHOICES

The United States Department of Agriculture (USDA) inspection sticker on poultry guarantees that it was raised and processed according to strict government guidelines. Grade A birds, the most common variety in supermarkets, are the highest quality. And more than 90 percent of all broiler-fryers are marketed under a brand name—a further assurance of quality.

ORGANIC The term organic is not recognized by the USDA, so it cannot appear on labels. The term can be used in advertisements to promote a brand, however. Generally, organic poultry has been raised on organically grown, antibiotic-free feed.

FREE-RANGE These birds have been raised in an environment that provides access to open spaces, but not necessarily an open farmyard. This free movement allows them to develop more muscle, which contributes to fuller-flavored meat.

ALL-NATURAL This simply means that the poultry has been minimally processed. Its feed was not necessarily organic and might have contained antibiotics.

KOSHER Birds have been processed according to kosher dietary laws under the strict supervision of a rabbi. The procedure includes salting to draw out the blood and season the meat.

HALAL If you live in an area that has a Muslim community, look for a halal butcher. These birds are not fed hormones and are processed manually while a special prayer is recited.

BUYING FRESH & FROZEN POULTRY

FRESH Look for fresh whole birds that appear plump and have meaty breasts. Chicken sold as parts should also look plump. Poultry skin should be smooth, moist, and free of bruises and pinfeathers. The color of the skin can range from creamy white to yellow, depending on the bird's feed and breed, and is not an indication of flavor or quality. In general, tenderness depends on the age of the bird.

•**Buy fresh poultry according to the "sell-by" date on the package.** When you open the package, the chicken may have a slight odor. This is caused by oxidation and should disappear in a few minutes. If the poultry still smells after a short time, return it to the market. Be sure to avoid packages with leaks or tears.

FROZEN If you buy frozen poultry, the meat should be rock-hard and without any signs of freezer burn. Make certain that there are no ice crystals on the poultry. The packaging should be tightly sealed and intact. Frozen liquid in the bottom may indicate that the bird was thawed and refrozen.

HANDLING & STORING POULTRY

•**Store raw poultry in its original store wrapping on a plate to catch any leaks.** If wrapped in butcher paper, remove the paper and place the bird in a large plastic bag. Keep poultry in the coldest part of the refrigerator (usually the bottom shelf towards the back), away from cooked or ready-to-eat foods, and use within two days. Store uncooked giblets separately in the refrigerator and use within a day, or wrap and freeze them for up to one month.

•**Don't rinse poultry.** Pat it dry with paper towels. If you remove chicken or turkey from its packaging in the sink, clear sponges, dishcloths, or anything that could catch juices before opening. Juices can cause cross-contamination.

•**Be sure to wash your hands**, the cutting board, and any utensils that have come in contact with raw poultry with hot, soapy water. To destroy germs, bleach your cutting board once a week or so with a solution of 1 tablespoon chlorine bleach to 1 gallon warm water.

•**Freeze raw poultry for up to six months.** Ground poultry will keep in the refrigerator for one day or in the freezer for up to three months. Cool cooked poultry as quickly as possible, then cover and refrigerate it up to three days, or tightly wrap and freeze it for up to three months. Make sure to date all packages before placing them in the freezer.

> **TIP**
>
> Cooking chicken with the skin adds flavor, not fat. The skin also helps retain juices in the meat, keeping it tender. The skin can be discarded after cooking if you are conscious of added fat, calories, and cholesterol in your diet.

PANCETTA CHICKEN
(PAGE 18)

THAWING POULTRY

•**For safety's sake,** thaw poultry either in the refrigerator or by immersion in cold water—not on the kitchen counter at room temperature.

THAWING IN THE REFRIGERATOR This is the preferred method. Leave the bird in its original wrapper and place it on a tray to catch any drips. As a general rule, allow about six hours per pound. For example a 4-pound chicken would take a full day to thaw.

THAWING IN COLD WATER If there's no time to thaw the bird in the refrigerator, use this method, which takes less time but requires more attention. Place the bird (in its original wrapper or in a watertight plastic bag) in a large pan or in the sink with enough cold water to cover. (Warm water thaws poultry too quickly and promotes bacterial growth.) Change the water every 30 minutes to maintain the temperature. Allow about 30 minutes of thawing time per pound, then add one hour to that total.

HOW TO CUT UP A RAW CHICKEN

TO REMOVE A LEG Using kitchen shears, cut down between the thigh and the body. Bend the leg portion back; twist to crack the hip joint. Cut through the joint. Repeat for the other leg.

TO SEPARATE THE LEG FROM THE THIGH Place the leg skin side down, and cut through the center joint with kitchen shears. Repeat with the other leg.

TO REMOVE A WING Pull the wing away from the body, then cut between the wing joint and the breast, using kitchen shears. Repeat with the other wing.

TO REMOVE THE BACKBONE Using kitchen shears, cut through the rib cage along one side of the backbone, from the tail to the neck. Repeat on the other side to remove the backbone in one piece.

TO REMOVE THE BREASTBONE Place the breast skin side down, and cut it in half by placing a heavy knife lengthwise along the center of the breastbone. Press the knife to cut through the bone and meat.

5 SAFE THAWING TIPS

1. Frozen poultry should be thawed completely before being cooked.

2. Remove giblets as soon as possible during thawing, then wrap and refrigerate.

3. A whole bird is thawed if the ice crystals have disappeared from the body cavity and the meat is soft.

4. Once thawed, cook the bird within 12 hours

5. For reasons of texture—not safety—do not refreeze thawed poultry.

REMOVING SKIN FROM CHICKEN

TO REMOVE THE SKIN FROM A CHICKEN THIGH
Grasp the skin tightly and pull it off in one piece. If you like, grasp the skin with a piece of paper towel or dip your fingers into a little coarse salt to get a better grip.

TO REMOVE THE SKIN FROM A DRUMSTICK
Grasp the skin at the meaty end of the drumstick; pull the skin down and off the end of the drumstick. (If necessary, use a sharp knife to cut the skin off.)

TO REMOVE THE SKIN FROM A CHICKEN BREAST Grasp the skin at the thin end of the breast and pull it off. (It is difficult to remove the skin from chicken wings—don't bother.)

NUTRITION STATS: HOW DOES YOUR FAVORITE CUT STACK UP?

•Boneless breast, the ultimate in high-quality, low-fat protein has only 165 calories for a 3½ ounce (100 grams) serving. Leave the skin on and you add about 30 calories, mostly fat.

•If you're a thigh fan 3½ ounces is 209 calories for the same portion (add another 20 calories for skin), you get a lot of flavor and less chance of dry chicken.

•Drumsticks come in at 175 calories for 3½ ounces (add another 40 calories for skin).

•A 3½-ounce portion of wings has 290 calories with skin on (if you manage to get the skin off, subtract 80 calories).

CARIBBEAN CHICKEN & "RICE" (PAGE 19)

POMEGRANATE-GLAZED CHICKEN (PAGE 23)

PAPRIKA CHICKEN
WITH TOMATOES
(PAGE 45)

1 | Weeknight Favorites

How many ways can you cook boneless chicken? This chapter will show you new ways to sauté, roast, stir-fry, steam, skewer, and poach the weeknight's friendliest cuts. Check out Lemony Chicken Soup, Fiery Kung Pao Chicken, Chicken Kabobs and Kale Caesar, Crispy Chicken Biscuits, and more. If you're a dark-meat fan, you can swap in boneless skinless thighs for most of the breast recipes (we take a scissors and snip any large fat pockets from the thighs before cooking).

Provençal Chicken Quinoa Bowls ··· 17

Pancetta Chicken ······················ 18

Caribbean Chicken & "Rice" ·········· 19

Chicken with Smoky Corn Salad ····· 21

Lighter Chicken Cacciatore ·········· 22

Pomegranate-Glazed Chicken ······· 23

Crispy Hot-Honey Chicken Sliders ·· 24

Fiery Kung Pao Chicken ··············· 25

Sesame Chicken Stir-Fry ············· 27

Spicy Chicken Miso Stir-Fry ········· 28

Chicken Coconut Curry ·············· 29

Cheesy Tex-Mex Stuffed Chicken ··· 31

Creamy Chicken-Corn Chowder ····· 33

Crispy Chicken Biscuits ·············· 35

Chicken Marsala Lite ················· 37

Lemony Chicken Soup ··············· 39

Chicken & Broccoli Packets ········· 40

Chicken & Broccoli Casserole ········ 41

Chicken Kebabs & Kale Caesar ······ 43

Prosciutto-Wrapped Chicken ········ 44

Paprika Chicken with Tomatoes ····· 45

Roasted Chicken & Tomatoes ········ 47

Chicken with Roasted Broccoli ······ 49

Chicken Cutlet Sammies ············· 51

Chicken with Creamy Spinach ······· 53

Chicken Roulade with Tomatoes ···· 55

Creamy Lemon Pasta with Chicken ···57

Provençal Chicken Quinoa Bowls

No herbes de Provence? This blend traditionally is thyme forward and includes oregano, savory fennel, and sometimes lavender and mint. Take a few pinches of each of these herbs from your spice rack.

PREP: 15 MINUTES   TOTAL: 25 MINUTES

4 chicken breast cutlets (about 5 ounces each)

¼ teaspoon herbes de Provence

Salt and ground black pepper

1 cup red quinoa

¼ cup Champagne vinegar

¼ cup olive oil

2 green onions

2 tablespoons Dijon mustard

4 cups packed arugula

12 ounces grape tomatoes, halved

⅔ cup pitted green olives, quartered

1. Season chicken-breast cutlets with herbes de Provence and ¼ teaspoon each salt and pepper.

2. Grill 3 minutes per side on medium-high or until cooked through (165°F).

3. Cook red quinoa according to package directions.

4. In blender, puree Champagne vinegar, olive oil, green onions, Dijon mustard, and ¼ teaspoon salt. Toss half the vinaigrette with cooked quinoa, arugula, grape tomatoes, and green olives.

5. Serve chicken over quinoa with remaining vinaigrette.

SERVES 4: About 500 calories, 36g protein, 35g carbohydrates, 23g fat (4g saturated), 8g fiber, 865mg sodium.

Pancetta Chicken

Wrapping the breasts in pancetta helps them retain their moisture.
If you prefer, you can swap in boneless, skinless thighs. See photo page 11.

See photo page 11.

PREP: 10 MINUTES   TOTAL: 40 MINUTES

**1½ pounds small skinless,
  boneless chicken-breast halves**

Salt

4 slices pancetta

Ground black pepper

1 pound green beans, trimmed

2 teaspoons olive oil

Lemon wedges

1. Preheat oven to 450°F.

2. Sprinkle chicken-breast halves with
½ teaspoon salt; drape 2 slices pancetta
over each one, tucking ends under.
Sprinkle with pepper.

3. Place on foil-lined, rimmed baking sheet.

4. On another baking sheet, toss green beans
with olive oil; season with salt and pepper.

5. Place baking sheets in oven; roast for 30
minutes or until chicken is cooked through
(165°F).

6. Serve together with lemon wedges.

SERVES 4: About 265 calories, 38g protein,
10g carbohydrates, 8g fat (2g saturated),
4g fiber, 520mg sodium.

Caribbean Chicken & "Rice"

The "rice" here is cauliflower. You can buy it prepared fresh
or frozen or pulse raw cauliflower in your food processor
until it's the size of rice grains. See photo page 13.

See photo page 13.

PREP: **10 MINUTES**   TOTAL: **30 MINUTES**

4 cups riced cauliflower

¼ cup water

4 skinless, boneless chicken-breast cutlets

2 teaspoons olive oil

Salt and ground black pepper

¼ cup sweetened cream of coconut

2 tablespoons hot sauce

2 limes, halved

1 (15-ounce) can black beans, rinsed and drained

Chopped cilantro, for garnish

1. Combine riced cauliflower and water; cover with vented plastic wrap and microwave on high 6 minutes.

2. Meanwhile, brush chicken-breast cutlets with olive oil; season all over with ½ teaspoon each salt and pepper. Grill on medium 5 minutes, turning over once halfway through. Whisk together sweetened cream of coconut and hot sauce; brush onto chicken. Grill until cooked through (165°F), about 5 minutes longer, brushing and turning 2 more times. Grill 2 limes, halved, until lightly charred, 2 to 3 minutes.

3. Toss cooked cauliflower with black beans, and ¼ teaspoon salt. Serve chicken over cauliflower with limes, garnished with chopped cilantro.

SERVES 4: About 370 calories, 37g protein, 37g carbohydrates, 9g fat (4g saturated), 10g fiber, 990 mg sodium.

Chicken with Smoky Corn Salad

The crunch of sweet corn pairs well with creamy Manchego and
briny olives for a balanced side to simple grilled chicken.

PREP: **10 MINUTES**   TOTAL: **30 MINUTES**

**4 (6-ounce) boneless, skinless
  chicken-breast halves**

Salt and ground black pepper

2 limes, halved

4 ears corn, shucked

¼ cup cilantro, chopped

2 tablespoons chopped green olives

1 ounce Manchego cheese, finely grated

1½ tablespoons olive oil

1 teaspoon smoked paprika

1. Preheat outdoor grill or 2-burner grill pan on medium-high.

2. Season chicken-breast halves with salt and pepper, and grill on medium-high to cook through (165°F), 5 to 6 minutes per side.

3. Meanwhile, grill 2 lime halves, cut side down, and corn until charred, 6 to 8 minutes. Turn corn to grill on all sides

4. Cut corn from cob and toss in bowl with juice of 2 lime halves. Then add cilantro, green olives, Manchego cheese, and a pinch each of salt and pepper.

5. Serve chicken with corn and remaining lime halves, and drizzle with a mixture of olive oil and smoked paprika.

SERVES 4: About 355 calories, 21g protein,
21g carbohydrates, 13g fat (3.5g saturated),
2g fiber, 315mg sodium.

Lighter Chicken Cacciatore

This quick take on an Italian-American favorite adds kale to the usual mushroom-and-pepper combo. Green olives and parsley add tang and freshness.

PREP: 30 MINUTES   TOTAL: 50 MINUTES

2 tablespoons olive oil

6 small boneless, skinless chicken breasts (5 ounces each)

Kosher salt and ground black pepper

10 ounces cremini mushrooms, quartered

1 small onion, thinly sliced

1 red pepper, thinly sliced

2 cloves garlic, finely chopped

2 teaspoons fresh rosemary, finely chopped

1 bay leaf

¾ cup dry white wine

1 (28-ounce) can diced tomatoes

8 ounces kale, stems discarded and leaves chopped

½ cup pitted green olives

¼ cup flat-leaf parsley, chopped

1. Heat oil in large deep skillet on medium-high. Season chicken with ½ teaspoon each salt and pepper, and cook until golden brown, 3 to 4 minutes per side; transfer to plate.

2. Add mushrooms and cook, tossing occasionally, until golden brown and tender, about 4 minutes. Transfer to plate with chicken.

3. Lower heat to medium and add onion, red pepper, garlic, rosemary, and bay leaf, and cook, stirring occasionally, until tender, 8 to 10 minutes. Add wine and cook, stirring and scraping up browned bits, until reduced by half, about 3 minutes. Stir in tomatoes (and their juices).

4. Return chicken and mushrooms to skillet, nestling chicken in tomatoes, and simmer, covered, for 15 minutes. Fold in kale and cook, covered, 10 to 12 minutes more. Uncover, discard bay leaf, and stir in olives and parsley.

SERVES 6: About 300 calories, 36g protein, 15g carbohydrates, 10g fat (1.5g saturated), 3g fiber, 690mg sodium.

> **TIP**
>
> Save time and buy pitted green olives.

Pomegranate-Glazed Chicken

The riot of color on the plate will perk up the darkest of winter days and the salt, sweet, and tang of this yummy glaze will do the same for your palate.

PREP: 10 MINUTES   TOTAL: 35 MINUTES

1 acorn squash, sliced ¾ inch thick, seeds removed

2 tablespoons olive oil

Kosher salt

Pinch of cayenne pepper

4 (6-ounce) skinless, boneless chicken breasts

¼ teaspoon ground black pepper

⅓ cup pomegranate juice

3 tablespoons honey

2 tablespoons balsamic vinegar

⅓ cup pomegranate seeds

⅓ cup crumbled feta

⅓ cup chopped mint

1. Preheat oven to 425°F.

2. On large rimmed baking sheet, toss acorn squash with 1 tablespoon olive oil, ½ teaspoon kosher salt, and pinch cayenne. Roast until tender, 20 to 25 minutes.

3. Meanwhile, heat 1 tablespoon oil in large skillet on medium. Season chicken breasts with ½ teaspoon kosher salt and ¼ teaspoon pepper; sauté until golden brown and cooked through (165°F), 4 to 6 minutes per side. Set chicken aside.

4. Cook pomegranate juice in same skillet on medium, stirring, 1 minute. Add honey and balsamic vinegar; simmer until thickened, 3 to 5 minutes.

5. Slice chicken; drizzle with glaze. Top squash with pomegranate seeds, crumbled feta, and chopped mint.

SERVES 4: About 440 calories, 42g protein, 38g carbohydrates, 14g fat (4g saturated), 6g fiber, 680mg sodium.

Crispy Hot-Honey Chicken Sliders

Crispy chicken sandwiches have become a popular fast food option.
We wanted to do an at-home version that's oven-baked (less fattening!).
A creamy slaw and a drizzle of must-have hot honey top it off.

TOTAL: 30 MINUTES

3 (8-ounce) boneless, skinless chicken breasts

4 cups cornflakes, coarsely crushed

½ cup buttermilk

½ teaspoon garlic powder

¼ teaspoon plus pinch cayenne pepper

Kosher salt

¼ cup sour cream

2 tablespoons cider vinegar

½ teaspoon poppy seeds

½ small napa cabbage, cored and thinly sliced (about 4 cups)

1 green onion, thinly sliced

12 (3-inch) pieces focaccia halved horizontally

Hot honey, for serving

1. Preheat oven to 425°F.

2. Line rimmed baking sheet with nonstick foil. Cut chicken in half horizontally to make thin pieces, then cut each piece in half crosswise.

3. Place cornflakes on plate. In medium bowl, combine ¼ cup buttermilk, garlic powder, ¼ teaspoon cayenne, and ½ teaspoon salt. Add chicken and toss to coat.

4. Working with 1 piece at a time, remove chicken, letting any excess buttermilk drip off, then coat in cornflakes, pressing gently to help them adhere. Transfer to prepared baking sheet. Roast, rotating pan once, until chicken is cooked through (165°F), 10 to 12 minutes.

5. Meanwhile, make slaw: In large bowl, whisk together sour cream, vinegar, poppy seeds, remaining ¼ cup buttermilk, pinch cayenne, and ¼ teaspoon salt. Add cabbage and toss to coat. Fold in green onions.

6. Form sandwiches with focaccia, chicken, slaw, and hot honey.

SERVES 12: About 250 calories, 17g protein, 31g carbohydrates, 6.5g fat (1.5g saturated), 2g fiber, 510mg sodium.

TIP

To make DIY hot honey, stir your favorite hot sauce into honey to your desired heat level.

Fiery Kung Pao Chicken

This take-out favorite is a cinch to make. Using thigh meat ensures that the chicken will stay moist and juicy.

PREP: 15 MINUTES   TOTAL: 30 MINUTES, PLUS MARINATING

¼ cup unsweetened rice wine

¼ cup soy sauce

1 tablespoon cornstarch

1½ pounds skinless, boneless chicken thighs, trimmed and cut into scant 1-inch chunks

1 tablespoon vegetable oil

1 bunch green onions, thinly sliced

3 cloves garlic, chopped

2 tablespoons finely chopped, peeled, fresh ginger

½ cup roasted unsalted peanuts

3 tablespoons balsamic vinegar

8 whole dried chilies de árbol

Cooked rice, for serving

Cilantro, for garnish

1. In medium bowl, whisk rice wine, soy sauce, and cornstarch until smooth. Add chicken; let stand 30 minutes or refrigerate up to 1 hour.

2. In 12-inch nonstick skillet, heat oil on medium-high. Add green onions, garlic, and ginger; cook 3 minutes or until garlic is golden brown, stirring. Add chicken and marinade; cook 3 to 5 minutes or until chicken is cooked through (165°F), stirring.

3. Stir in peanuts, vinegar, and chilies; cook 2 minutes, stirring. Serve with rice, garnished with cilantro.

SERVES 6: About 260 calories, 27g protein, 9g carbohydrates, 13g fat (2g saturated), 2g fiber, 700mg sodium.

TIP

If someone in your family has a peanut allergy, you can use toasted, slivered almonds.

Sesame Chicken Stir-Fry

This satisfying homestyle stir-fry hits all the sweet, hot, and tangy notes—
and it can be on the table in less time than it takes to get delivery!

TOTAL: 20 MINUTES

1 cup rice

2 tablespoons canola oil

1 red pepper, roughly chopped

1 yellow pepper, roughly chopped

1 onion, roughly chopped

1 pound boneless, skinless chicken breasts,
cut into 1-inch pieces

3 tablespoons cornstarch

1 tablespoon canola oil

2 tablespoons low-sodium soy sauce

2 tablespoons rice vinegar

1 tablespoon sriracha

1 tablespoon honey

1 teaspoon toasted sesame oil

2 cloves garlic, finely chopped

1 (1-inch) piece fresh ginger,
peeled and finely chopped

⅓ cup water

1 tablespoon toasted sesame seeds

2 green onions, thinly sliced

1. Cook 1 cup rice according to package directions. Heat 1 tablespoon canola oil in large nonstick skillet on medium. Add red pepper, yellow pepper, and onion, and cook, stirring occasionally, until tender, 6 to 8 minutes; transfer to bowl.

2. Meanwhile, in large bowl, toss the chicken breasts with cornstarch.

3. Add 1 tablespoon canola oil to same skillet and cook chicken, stirring occasionally, until golden and cooked through (165°F), 5 to 7 minutes.

4. Meanwhile, in bowl, mix soy sauce, rice vinegar, sriracha, honey, and sesame oil. Stir in garlic and ginger.

5. Return vegetables to pan, then add sauce and water; simmer until slightly thickened, about 2 minutes. Sprinkle with toasted sesame seeds and green onions. Serve over rice.

SERVES 4: About 495 calories, 32g protein, 60g carbohydrates, 13g fat (1.5g saturated), 3g fiber, 425mg sodium.

Spicy Chicken Miso Stir-Fry

Miso paste, made from fermented soybeans, is one of those magical umami ingredients that can transform a dish from everyday to WOW.

PREP: 15 MINUTES   TOTAL: 25 MINUTES

2 cloves garlic, chopped

2 serrano chilies, thinly sliced

1 tablespoon chopped, peeled fresh ginger

2 tablespoons vegetable oil

1¼ pounds skinless, boneless chicken breasts, cut into ½-inch chunks

Salt and ground black pepper

2 tablespoons yellow or white miso

2 tablespoons water

4 green onions, sliced

3 cups cooked, riced cauliflower

1. In 12-inch skillet on medium, cook garlic, chilies, and ginger in vegetable oil, 3 minutes or until garlic is golden, stirring.

2. Add chicken breasts and ¼ teaspoon each salt and pepper. Cook 4 minutes.

3. In small bowl, whisk yellow or white miso and water until smooth; add to skillet along with green onions. Cook 3 minutes or until chicken is cooked through (165°F), stirring occasionally. Serve with cooked riced cauliflower.

SERVES 4: About 285 calories, 36g protein, 9g carbohydrates, 12g fat (1g saturated), 3g fiber, 595mg sodium.

TIP

Miso paste is available in white, red, and mixed. The lighter the color of the paste, the sweeter and milder the flavor.

Chicken Coconut Curry

You'll want plenty of rice or flatbread to sop up this delicious sauce. If you can't find cashew butter, use almond butter in its place.

3 tablespoons olive oil

2 pounds boneless, skinless chicken breasts, cut into 1-inch chunks

Kosher salt and ground black pepper

1 large onion, chopped

4 cloves garlic, pressed

1 red chili, finely chopped

1 (2-inch) piece fresh ginger, peeled and coarsely grated

1 tablespoon garam masala

1 (28-ounce) can crushed tomatoes

¾ cup coconut milk

½ cup cashew butter

Cooked rice, cilantro, chopped cashews, and sliced red chilies, for serving (optional)

1. Heat 2 tablespoons oil in large Dutch oven on medium. Season chicken with ½ teaspoon each salt and pepper, and cook, tossing often, until no longer pink, 5 minutes; transfer to bowl.

2. Reduce heat to medium-low; add remaining tablespoon oil, then onion, and cook, covered, stirring occasionally, until tender and beginning to brown, 6 to 8 minutes. Stir in garlic and chilies and cook 1 minute. Stir in ginger, garam masala, and ½ teaspoon salt and cook 1 minute.

3. Add tomatoes, coconut milk, and cashew butter, and mix to combine. Return chicken and any juices to pot and gently simmer, covered, stirring occasionally, until chicken is cooked through (165°F), 6 to 8 minutes. Serve over rice, topped with cilantro, cashews, and chilies, if desired.

SERVES 6: About 485 calories, 41g protein, 21g carbohydrates, 28g fat (9.5g saturated), 4g fiber, 645mg sodium.

Cheesy Tex-Mex Stuffed Chicken

This luscious chicken packs some heat! For a milder version, use only one jalapeño pepper. Desire more heat? Substitute pepper jack cheese.

PREP: **20 MINUTES**   TOTAL: **30 MINUTES**

2 green onions, thinly sliced

2 seeded jalapeño peppers, thinly sliced

¼ cup cilantro, chopped

1 teaspoon lime zest

4 ounces Monterey Jack cheese, coarsely grated

4 small boneless, skinless chicken breasts

3 tablespoons olive oil

Salt and ground black pepper

3 tablespoons lime juice

2 bell peppers, thinly sliced

½ small red onion, thinly sliced

5 cups torn romaine lettuce

1 cup fresh cilantro

Lime wedges, for serving

1. Preheat oven to 450°F.

2. In bowl, combine green onions and jalapeño peppers, cilantro, and lime zest, then toss with Monterey Jack cheese.

3. Insert knife into thickest part of each of the chicken breasts and move back and forth to create 2½-inch pocket that is as wide as possible without going through. Stuff chicken with cheese mixture.

4. Heat 2 tablespoons olive oil in large ovenproof skillet on medium. Season chicken with salt and pepper, and cook until golden brown on 1 side, 3 to 4 minutes. Turn chicken over. Place skillet in oven and roast until chicken is cooked through (165°F), 10 to 12 minutes.

5. Meanwhile, in large bowl, whisk together lime juice, 1 tablespoon olive oil, and ½ teaspoon salt. Add bell peppers and red onion, and let sit 10 minutes, tossing occasionally. Toss with romaine lettuce and cilantro. Serve with chicken and lime wedges.

SERVES 4: About 360 calories, 32g protein, 0g carbohydrates, 22g fat (7.5g saturated), 3g fiber, 715mg sodium.

Creamy Chicken-Corn Chowder

Sweet tarragon is a delicious match for the corn.
Basil would also be a yummy option.

PREP: 15 MINUTES   TOTAL: 1 HOUR 5 MINUTES

4 large ears corn, shucked

2½ pounds bone-in chicken breasts,
  skin removed

8 cups water

Salt

4 tablespoons butter

1 tablespoon olive oil

5 stalks celery, chopped

4 large carrots, chopped

1 medium onion, finely chopped

⅓ cup all-purpose flour

½ cup half-and-half

3 tablespoons fresh tarragon leaves,
  chopped

Ground black pepper

1. Cut corn kernels from cobs; set kernels aside. Scrape juices from cobs into 5- to 6-quart saucepot; add cobs, along with chicken, water, and ½ teaspoon salt. Heat to boiling on high. Reduce heat to maintain gentle simmer. Cook 20 to 25 minutes or until chicken is cooked, turning chicken breasts occasionally. Remove pot from heat and let cool. Transfer chicken to large bowl. When cool enough to handle, remove and discard any bones; pull meat into bite-size pieces. Remove and discard cobs from poaching liquid; reserve liquid.

2. Meanwhile, in 7- to 8-quart saucepot, heat butter and oil on medium until butter has melted. Add celery, carrots, onions, and ½ teaspoon salt. Cook 10 minutes or until beginning to soften, stirring frequently.

3. Sprinkle flour over vegetables; cook 1 minute, stirring. Stir in reserved poaching liquid and corn kernels. Heat to boiling on high; boil 1 minute, stirring. Reduce heat to maintain simmer. Cook 15 minutes, stirring occasionally. Stir in half-and-half, tarragon, reserved chicken, 1 teaspoon salt, and ½ teaspoon pepper.

SERVES 8: About 300 calories, 25g protein, 24g carbohydrates, 13g fat (6g saturated), 3g fiber, 645mg sodium.

Crispy Chicken Biscuits

Tossing the chicken in ranch dressing adds a flavor
burst and helps the cornflake crust to stick.

1 pound boneless, skinless chicken breasts

¼ cup ranch dressing

½ teaspoon cayenne

½ teaspoon garlic powder

1 tablespoon water

Kosher salt

4 cups cornflakes

6 biscuits

Lettuce, hot sauce, and salad,
  for serving (optional)

1. Preheat oven to 425°F.

2. Line rimmed baking sheet with nonstick foil.
Cut chicken in half crosswise, then cut thicker
half in half again horizontally to create 3 pieces
of even thickness.

3. In medium bowl, combine ranch, cayenne,
garlic powder, water, and ¼ teaspoon salt. Toss
chicken pieces in ranch mixture, then coat with
cornflakes, pressing gently to adhere.

4. Arrange chicken on prepared baking sheet
and bake, rotating pan once, until chicken is
cooked through (165°F), 10 to 12 minutes.

5. Form sandwiches with biscuits, chicken,
lettuce, and hot sauce, if desired. Serve chicken
biscuits with a salad, if desired.

SERVES 6: About 402 calories, 21g protein,
41g carbohydrates, 17g fat (8g saturated),
2g fiber, 898mg sodium.

TIP

No ranch in the house? No problem. Whisk
together 1 tablespoon mayo, 2 tablespoons
milk, 1 tablespoon white vinegar or lemon
juice, and a pinch of salt and black pepper.

Chicken Marsala Lite

Cremini mushrooms, which are baby portabellas, add a rich earthy flavor to this dish. You can swap in any type of mushrooms if you prefer.

PREP: 5 MINUTES   TOTAL: 30 MINUTES

4 (6-ounce) boneless, skinless chicken breasts

Salt and ground black pepper

Flour

2 tablespoons olive oil

1 (10-ounce) package sliced cremini mushrooms

1 large shallot, finely chopped

1 clove garlic, finely chopped

½ cup low-sodium chicken broth

½ cup Marsala wine

Chopped parsley

Sautéed spinach, for serving

1. Pound 4 (6-ounce) boneless, skinless chicken breasts to ½ inch thick. Season with salt and pepper and lightly coat with flour. Heat 1 tablespoon olive oil in large skillet on medium, and cook chicken until golden brown, 4 to 5 minutes per side; transfer to plate.

2. Add 1 tablespoon oil to skillet. Cook sliced cremini mushrooms on medium-high, tossing occasionally, until golden brown, 5 minutes. Add shallots and garlic. Season with salt and pepper; cook 2 minutes.

3. Add chicken broth and Marsala wine to skillet, along with chicken and juices, and simmer until reduced by half, 4 minutes, and until chicken is cooked through (165°F). Sprinkle with chopped parsley. Serve with sautéed spinach.

SERVES 4: About 355 calories, 42g protein, 14g carbohydrates, 11.5g fat (2g saturated), 1g fiber, 335mg sodium.

TIP

Marsala, Italy's most famous fortified wine, is produced by a process similar to the one used in Spain to make sherry. Marsala is made in several different styles: secco (dry), semisecco (semisweet), and dolce (sweet). It is also classified based on its flavor characteristics and aging. When cooking, we recommend dry or semi-dry styles.

Lemony Chicken Soup

Greek avgolemono soup morphs into a main dish with
the addition of poached chicken and spinach.

PREP: **25 MINUTES**   TOTAL: **1 HOUR**

2 large yellow onions, halved

1 head garlic, halved

1 rind Parmesan

12 cups water

Kosher salt and ground black pepper

1¼ pounds small, boneless, skinless
   chicken breasts

2 large eggs

6 tablespoons fresh lemon juice

6 cups baby spinach

1. In large pot, simmer onions, garlic, Parmesan rind, and water for 25 minutes; strain. Season with ½ teaspoon each salt and pepper and return to a simmer. Add chicken and poach until cooked through (165°F), 11 to 13 minutes. Then, using tongs, transfer chicken to bowl (do not discard broth). Let cool slightly and shred into pieces.

2. Meanwhile, in medium bowl, whisk together eggs and lemon juice until foamy. Slowly, 1 tablespoon at a time, whisk in 1 cup broth from pot. Whisking broth in pot constantly, slowly add egg broth mixture to pot. Reduce heat to medium-low and cook until soup is slightly thickened and velvety, about 5 minutes. Remove from heat, stir in chicken and spinach, and let sit 5 minutes.

SERVES 4: About 270 calories, 38g protein, 14g carbohydrates, 6.5g fat (1.5g saturated), 4g fiber, 410mg sodium.

Chicken & Broccoli Packets

Cooking in parchment paper keeps flavors and moisture
locked in—plus it's fast and healthy!

PREP: 35 MINUTES   TOTAL: 45 MINUTES

1¼ pounds broccoli, stems sliced, crowns cut
into small florets

2 cloves garlic, pressed

2 tablespoons olive oil

Kosher salt and ground black pepper

4 (6-ounce) boneless, skinless chicken breasts

1 lemon

½ small red onion, finely chopped

8 ounces tomatoes, chopped

1. Preheat oven to 400°F.

2. Toss broccoli with garlic, 1 tablespoon oil,
and ¼ teaspoon each salt and pepper. Divide
among four 12-inch squares of parchment.
Season chicken with ¼ teaspoon each salt and
pepper and place on top of broccoli. Cover with
a second piece of parchment and fold up edges
to seal. Place packets on 2 rimmed baking
sheets and roast 15 minutes.

3. Meanwhile, finely grate zest of lemon and
squeeze 2 tablespoons of lemon juice. In
medium bowl, combine onions, lemon juice,
remaining tablespoon oil, and ¼ teaspoon each
salt and pepper. Let sit 4 minutes, then toss
with tomatoes. Cut open parchment packets;
top with salad and lemon zest.

SERVES 4: About 330 calories, 43g protein,
14g carbohydrates, 12g fat (2g saturated),
5g fiber, 485mg sodium.

Chicken & Broccoli Casserole

This update of classic Chicken Divan features a creamy
Parmesan sauce instead of Cheddar.

PREP: 20 MINUTES   TOTAL: 40 MINUTES

1 pound boneless, skinless chicken breasts

Kosher salt and ground black pepper

1 tablespoon plus 1 teaspoon olive oil

1 yellow onion, finely chopped

1 clove garlic, pressed

3 tablespoons all-purpose flour

3 ounces Parmesan, finely grated

12 ounces broccoli florets

3 ounces roughly torn baguette
   (about 2 cups)

1. Preheat oven to 425°F.

2. Cut chicken into 1½-inch pieces; season
with ½ teaspoon each salt and pepper. Heat
1 tablespoon oil in large skillet on medium-
high, and cook chicken until browned on 1 side,
about 2 minutes; transfer to plate. Reduce heat
to medium-low, then add onions; sauté until
tender, 5 minutes. Stir in garlic; cook 1 minute.

3. Sprinkle flour over onions and cook,
stirring, 1 minute. Slowly stir in 1½ cups
water, scraping up any browned bits, then
Parmesan. In 2½-quart shallow baking dish,
toss together chicken and broccoli. Spoon
onion mixture over top and bake 10 minutes.

4. Meanwhile, in food processor, pulse baguette
with remaining teaspoon oil to form coarse
crumbs; sprinkle over casserole and bake until
golden brown, about 15 minutes.

SERVES 4: About 375 calories, 37g protein,
25g carbohydrates, 14g fat (4.5g saturated),
3g fiber, 800mg sodium.

Chicken Kebabs & Kale Caesar

This punchy dressing pairs well with rich, grilled chicken and hearty kale. If you're an anchovy fan, mash a couple fillets and add them to the dressing, along with the lemon juice.

TOTAL: 25 MINUTES

2 lemons

1½ pounds boneless, skinless chicken breasts

Kosher salt and ground black pepper

8 thick slices baguette or artisanal bread

1 clove garlic, halved, plus ½ small clove garlic, finely grated

1 large egg yolk

½ teaspoon Dijon mustard

⅓ cup olive oil

¼ cup grated Parmesan

5 ounces baby kale

1. Preheat outdoor grill or 2-burner grill pan on medium-high.

2. Cut 1 lemon in half. From remaining lemon, finely grate 1 teaspoon zest and squeeze 4 tablespoons juice.

3. Cut chicken into 1½-inch chunks; thread onto skewers and season with ¼ teaspoon each salt and pepper. Grill until cooked through (165°F), 3 to 4 minutes per side. Grill 1 lemon half, cut side down, until charred; squeeze over chicken. Grill bread until toasted, rub both sides with garlic halves, then cut bread into cubes. Discard garlic halves.

4. In bowl, whisk together lemon juice and zest, egg yolk, mustard, grated garlic, and ½ teaspoon salt. Slowly whisk in oil. Fold in Parmesan, then kale and croutons, and season with pepper. Serve with chicken.

SERVES 4: About 465 calories, 41g protein, 18g carbohydrates, 25g fat (5g saturated), 2g fiber, 705mg sodium.

Prosciutto-Wrapped Chicken

In this easy sheet pan supper, the prosciutto seasons the chicken and crisps up, and the squash is a sweet counterpoint to the savory thyme. Serve with steamed green beans or broccoli on the side, if you like.

PREP: 10 MINUTES   TOTAL: 45 MINUTES

2 small acorn squash, seeded and sliced

2 tablespoons olive oil

2 teaspoons fresh thyme leaves

Salt

4 skinless, boneless chicken thighs (about 1¼ pounds in all)

Ground black pepper

3 tablespoons grated Parmesan

4 slices prosciutto

Sautéed green beans, for serving

1. Preheat oven to 450°F.

2. On large rimmed baking sheet, toss the acorn squash with olive oil, thyme leaves, and ½ teaspoon salt. Roast 35 minutes or until tender.

3. Season chicken thighs with ½ teaspoon pepper; sprinkle with Parmesan. Wrap each with 1 slice prosciutto. Arrange chicken on foil-lined, rimmed baking sheet. Bake 25 minutes or until cooked through (165°F).

4. Serve chicken and squash with sautéed green beans.

SERVES 4: About 375 calories, 32g protein, 24g carbohydrates, 18g fat (4g saturated), 5g fiber, 755mg sodium.

TIP

Can you eat the skin of acorn squash? Absolutely—it's totally edible and tasty. Plus, it's high in fiber!

Paprika Chicken with Tomatoes

Oh, how we love a sheet pan dinner! This Spanish-inspired one
is short on ingredients but has lasting flavor. If you like, swap
in 1 teaspoon of smoked paprika. See photo on page 14.

PREP: 15 MINUTES   TOTAL: 20 MINUTES

12 ounces tomatoes

8 cloves garlic, smashed, in their skins

1 (15-ounce) can chickpeas, rinsed

3 tablespoons olive oil

Kosher salt and ground black pepper

4 (6-ounce) boneless, skinless chicken breasts

2 teaspoons paprika

1. Preheat oven to 425°F.

2. On rimmed baking sheet, toss tomatoes, garlic, and chickpeas with 2 tablespoons oil and ¼ teaspoon each salt and pepper. Roast 10 minutes.

3. Heat remaining tablespoon oil in large skillet on medium. Season chicken with paprika and ½ teaspoon each salt and pepper, and cook until golden brown on one side, 5 to 6 minutes. Flip and cook 1 minute more or until chicken is cooked through (165°F).

4. Transfer to baking sheet with tomatoes and chickpeas, and roast until cooked through, 6 minutes more.

5. Before serving, discard garlic skins.

SERVES 4: About 390 calories, 40g protein, 21g carbohydrates, 16g fat (2.5g saturated), 6g fiber, 590mg sodium.

Roasted Chicken & Tomatoes

Get out your big cast-iron skillet for this one—it crisps the chicken skin beautifully. Don't be tempted to use balsamic in this recipe: The bright flavor of red wine vinegar is a well-suited match for sweet fennel seeds.

PREP: 10 MINUTES   TOTAL: 25 MINUTES

1 teaspoon and 1 tablespoon oil

2 large bone-in chicken breasts, about 12 ounces each

Salt and ground black pepper

1 pound cherry tomatoes, halved

1 sprig rosemary

1 teaspoon fennel seeds, crushed

1 cup instant polenta

1 teaspoon red wine vinegar

¼ cup parsley, chopped

1. Preheat oven to 450°F.

2. Heat 1 teaspoon oil in large, oven-safe skillet on medium. Season chicken breasts with ½ teaspoon each salt and pepper. Cook, skin side down, until golden brown and crisp, 5 to 7 minutes.

3. Turn; add cherry tomatoes, rosemary, and fennel seeds. Drizzle with 1 tablespoon oil, season with ¼ teaspoon each salt and pepper, then roast until chicken is just cooked through (165°F) and tomatoes have begun to break down, 12 to 15 minutes. Remove from the oven.

4. Meanwhile, prepare instant polenta according to package directions.

5. Discard rosemary from the skillet; transfer chicken to cutting board and let rest 5 minutes. Stir red wine vinegar into tomatoes, then toss with parsley. Remove bone from chicken, slice, and serve on polenta. Top with tomatoes.

SERVES 4: About 445 calories, 32g protein, 37g carbohydrates, 17.5g fat (4g saturated), 3g fiber, 455mg sodium.

TIP

Transfer leftover polenta to a loaf pan and refrigerate until set. Slice, then pan-fry and serve with an egg and leftover tomatoes.

Chicken with Roasted Broccoli

Using the skillet and sheet pan saves time, and gives
optimum results to this citrusy dish.

PREP: 25 MINUTES   TOTAL: 30 MINUTES

1½ pounds broccoli, cut into florets

2 cloves garlic, thinly sliced

3 tablespoons olive oil

Kosher salt and ground black pepper

4 (6-ounce) boneless, skinless
 chicken breasts

¼ cup all-purpose flour

1 lemon, cut into ½-inch pieces,
 plus 2 tablespoons lemon juice

⅓ cup water

1. Preheat oven to 425°F.

2. On rimmed baking sheet, toss broccoli and garlic with 1 tablespoon oil and ¼ teaspoon each salt and pepper; roast 10 minutes.

3. Meanwhile, pound chicken breasts to even thickness, season with ¼ teaspoon each salt and pepper, then coat in flour. Heat 1 tablespoon oil in large skillet on medium-high and cook chicken until golden brown, 3 to 5 minutes per side.

4. Nestle chicken amid broccoli and roast until chicken is cooked through (165°F) and broccoli is golden brown and tender, about 6 minutes.

5. Meanwhile, return skillet to medium heat; add remaining tablespoon oil, then lemon pieces, and cook, stirring, until beginning to brown, 3 minutes. Add lemon juice and water and cook, stirring and scraping up any browned bits. Spoon over chicken and serve with broccoli.

SERVES 4: About 365 calories, 44g protein, 15g carbohydrates, 15.5g fat (2.5g saturated), 5g fiber, 375mg sodium.

Chicken Cutlet Sammies

Pickled onions and wilted spinach star in these juicy chicken sandwiches.
Add a few slices of Provolone cheese to the toasting bread, if you like.

TOTAL: **20 MINUTES**

½ small red onion, thinly sliced

1 tablespoon red wine vinegar

Kosher salt and ground black pepper

1 pound boneless, skinless chicken breasts

1 tablespoon olive oil

6 cups baby spinach

4 (5-inch) pieces baguette,
   split and toasted

1. Toss onion with vinegar and ⅛ teaspoon
each salt and pepper; let sit.

2. Cut chicken into 6 thin cutlets. Heat oil in
large skillet on medium-high. Season chicken
with ½ teaspoon each salt and pepper, and cook
until browned and cooked through (165°F),
2 minutes per side; transfer to cutting board.

3. Add spinach to skillet, season with salt and
pepper, and cook until just beginning to wilt.
Slice chicken and sandwich between baguette
halves with spinach and onions.

***

SERVES 4: About 330 calories, 33g protein,
32g carbohydrates 7g fat (1g saturated),
3g fiber, 705mg sodium.

Chicken with Creamy Spinach

If you're a fan of hot artichoke dip, this one's for you! Egg noodles would make a good side dish for this creamy sauce.

PREP: 10 MINUTES   TOTAL: 30 MINUTES

4 (6-ounce) boneless, skinless chicken breasts

Salt and ground black pepper

2 tablespoons oil

1 lemon

1 (14-ounce) can artichoke hearts

2 cloves garlic, thinly sliced

½ cup dry white wine

¼ cup sour cream

1 bunch spinach leaves

1. Season chicken breasts with ½ teaspoon each salt and pepper. In skillet on medium, cook chicken in 1 tablespoon oil, 6 to 8 minutes per side. Remove from heat and squeeze juice of 1 lemon on top.

2. Meanwhile, halve artichoke hearts, place them cut side down in the same skillet, and cook in 1 tablespoon oil on medium-high, 3 minutes.

3. Lower heat to medium; toss with garlic. Stir in white wine; cook 2 minutes. Stir in sour cream and spinach leaves; season with salt and pepper, and cook until just wilted.

4. Serve the chicken alongside creamy spinach and artichokes and enjoy.

SERVES 4: About 305 calories, 38g protein, 10g carbohydrates, 11.5g fat (3g saturated), 2g fiber, 675mg sodium.

Chicken Roulade with Tomatoes

Roulades always look so impressive, and they're pretty easy to pull off (though you don't need to admit this to your guests). When local heirloom tomatoes are in season, quarter and slice a few varieties.

TOTAL: 35 MINUTES

4 boneless, skinless chicken breasts

2 cloves garlic, finely grated

2 tablespoons lemon zest, plus 2 tablespoons lemon juice

½ cup finely grated Parmesan

32 baby spinach leaves

Kosher salt and ground black pepper

3 tablespoons olive oil

2 pints grape or cherry tomatoes, sliced

¼ small red onion, thinly sliced

2 tablespoons red wine vinegar

1. Preheat oven to 450°F.

2. Pound chicken breasts into thin cutlets.

3. In small bowl, combine garlic, lemon zest, and Parmesan.

4. Lay 8 spinach leaves on each chicken cutlet, then sprinkle garlic mixture on top. Roll chicken up and secure with a toothpick (place toothpick parallel to seam to make turning roulades easier). Season chicken with ½ teaspoon each salt and pepper.

5. Heat 1 tablespoon oil in large ovenproof skillet on medium-high. Carefully add roulades, seam side down, and cook, turning until browned on all sides, 6 to 7 minutes. Transfer to oven and bake until cooked through (165°F), 8 to 9 minutes more. Drizzle lemon juice on roulades.

6. While chicken roasts, toss together tomatoes, onion, red wine vinegar, remaining 2 tablespoons oil, and ½ teaspoon each salt and pepper. Serve with chicken.

SERVES 4: About 310 calories, 31g protein, 10g carbohydrates, 16.5g fat (4g saturated), 3g fiber, 735mg sodium.

Creamy Lemon Pasta with Chicken

Pasta with lemon is a classic from the Amalfi Coast, which is famous for its flavorful citrus. Adding chicken turns this into a delicious main dish.

PREP: 10 MINUTES   TOTAL: 25 MINUTES

2 tablespoons olive oil

12 ounces boneless, skinless chicken breasts, cut into 2-inch pieces

Kosher salt and ground black pepper

¼ cup fresh lemon juice

4 cups low-sodium chicken broth

12 ounces gemelli or other short pasta

4 ounces cream cheese, at room temperature

1 cup peas, thawed if frozen

2 teaspoons lemon zest

½ cup finely grated Parmesan

1 tablespoon finely chopped tarragon

1. Heat oil in large, deep skillet on medium-high. Season chicken with ¼ teaspoon each salt and pepper, and cook until golden brown on all sides, 4 to 5 minutes; transfer to large bowl. Add lemon juice to pan, scraping up browned bits, then pour over chicken in bowl.

2. Add broth and pasta to skillet, and bring to a boil. Reduce heat and simmer, stirring often, 10 minutes.

3. Return chicken (and any juices) to skillet and continue to cook until pasta is just tender, about 3 minutes.

4. Add cream cheese, stirring to melt, then fold in peas, lemon zest, Parmesan, and tarragon.

SERVES 4: About 675 calories, 41g protein, 75g carbohydrates, 23.5g fat (9g saturated), 5g fiber, 535mg sodium.

QUICK CHICKEN MOLE
(PAGE 66)

2 | Bone-in Chicken

The bones have it—flavor that is. For keeping it simple, nothing beats the easy prep and big flavors of sheet pan roasts, like Fennel Roasted Chicken & Peppers and Honey Mustard–Glazed Chicken Bake. Less than half an hour in a hot oven and you've got dinner. Plus, the Instant Pot does a delicious job on bone-in parts, using either the pressure or slow-cook mode. Try Quicker Coq au Vin Blanc or Slow-Cooker Tex-Mex Soup with all the fixings. Need a crispy, spicy fix? Fry up our irresistible Nashville Hot Chicken.

Skillet Lemon Chicken with Artichokes · 60

Slow-Cooker Tex-Mex Soup · · · · · · · · 61

Crispy Chicken with White Wine Pan Sauce · 63

Nashville Hot Chicken · · · · · · · · · · · · · · · 64

Buttermilk Fried Chicken · · · · · · · · · · · 65

Quick Chicken Mole · · · · · · · · · · · · · · · · · 66

Crunchy Deviled Chicken · · · · · · · · · · · 67

Sheet Pan Chickpea Chicken · · · · · · · · 69

Moroccan Chicken with Preserved Lemons & Olives · · · · · · · · · · 70

Quicker Coq au Vin Blanc · · · · · · · · · · · · 71

Spicy Jerk Drumsticks · · · · · · · · · · · · · · · 73

Honey Mustard–Glazed Chicken Bake · 75

Fennel Roasted Chicken & Peppers · · · 77

Skillet Pesto Chicken & Beans · · · · · · · 79

Grilled Chicken with White BBQ Sauce · 80

Mushroom Chicken Skillet with Herbed Cream Sauce · · · · · · · · · · · · 81

Spiced Sesame Chicken with Carrots & Couscous · · · · · · · · · · · · · · · · · 83

Sweet & Sticky Chicken with Snow Peas · 85

Skillet Lemon Chicken with Artichokes

Canned artichoke hearts require no further cooking. If you want to use frozen or fresh ones, cook them separately first. See photo page 2.

PREP: 10 MINUTES   TOTAL: 25 MINUTES

1 teaspoon oil

6 small chicken thighs
(about 2 pounds)

Salt and ground black pepper

1 medium onion, chopped

⅔ cup dry white wine

1 tablespoon butter

1 (14-ounce) can artichoke hearts,
rinsed, drained, and quartered

1 medium lemon, thinly sliced
and seeded

Chopped parsley, for garnish

Steamed rice, for serving

1. Preheat oven to 450°F.

2. In 12-inch skillet, heat oil on medium-high. Season chicken thighs with ½ teaspoon each salt and pepper. Place skin side down; cook 5 to 8 minutes or until golden brown. Transfer chicken, skin side up, to rimmed, foil-lined baking sheet and roast 15 minutes or until cooked through (165°F).

3. To same skillet on medium, add onion and ¼ teaspoon salt. Cook 3 minutes, stirring. Add white wine and simmer 2 minutes, scraping up any browned bits. Stir in butter until melted, then artichoke hearts and lemon.

4. To serve, spoon sauce over chicken; garnish with chopped parsley. Serve with steamed rice.

SERVES 4: About 510 calories, 34g protein, 10g carbohydrates, 36g fat (11g saturated), 1g fiber, 790mg sodium.

TIP

Fresh mint would be a tasty alternative to the parsley in this recipe.

Slow-Cooker Tex-Mex Soup

Don't skimp on the garnishes: Tortilla strips add crunch and avocado lends even more creaminess. Serve with more lime if you like.

PREP: 20 MINUTES   TOTAL: 4 HOURS 20 MINUTES

2½ pounds bone-in, skin-on chicken thighs, skin removed

4 cups low-sodium chicken broth

3 large stalks celery, sliced

3 medium carrots, sliced

2 poblano peppers, seeded and chopped

1 medium onion, chopped

3 cloves garlic, chopped

1 tablespoon ground cumin

1 tablespoon ground coriander

2 (15-ounce) cans white (cannellini) beans, drained

Salt

8 ounces Monterey Jack cheese, shredded

2 tablespoons lime juice

Chopped avocado, cilantro leaves, sour cream, and Baked Tortilla Strips (recipe at right), for garnish (optional)

1. To 6- to 7-quart slow-cooker bowl, add chicken, broth, celery, carrots, peppers, onions, garlic, cumin, coriander, beans, and ½ teaspoon salt. Cover and cook on low 4 to 5 hours or until carrots are tender.

2. Remove and discard bones from chicken; shred chicken and return to slow-cooker bowl.

3. Add cheese, lime juice, and ¼ teaspoon salt to soup in bowl, stirring until cheese melts. Serve topped with avocado, cilantro, sour cream, and Baked Tortilla Strips, if desired.

SERVES 6 (soup only): About 445 calories, 40g protein, 34g carbohydrates, 16g fat (7g saturated), 14g fiber, 1,070mg sodium.

Baked Tortilla Strips

Preheat the oven to 425°. Stack **4 small corn tortillas;** thinly slice into ⅛-inch-wide strips. Arrange in a single layer on large baking sheet. Spray all over with **nonstick cooking spray**. Bake 4 to 5 minutes or until deep golden brown. Let cool completely.

TIP

Want to prepare this dish ahead of time? Proceed with Slow-Cooker Tex-Mex Soup recipe through step 2. Hold on slow cooker's keep warm setting up to 3 hours or transfer to container and refrigerate, covered, up to 2 days; reheat in pot on stovetop on medium-high, about 15 minutes or until simmering. Continue with step 3.

Crispy Chicken with White Wine Pan Sauce

Searing then baking the chicken ensures crispy skin. Plus, you can compose this luscious pan sauce while the chicken cooks.

2 teaspoons olive oil

2½ pounds chicken thighs

Salt

2 medium shallots, chopped

⅔ cup white wine

¼ teaspoon dried rosemary

3 tablespoons low-fat sour cream

½ cup chicken broth

Snipped chives, for garnish

1. Preheat oven to 450°F.

2. In 12-inch skillet, heat olive oil on medium-high. Season chicken thighs with ½ teaspoon salt. Cook, skin side down, 6 to 8 minutes or until browned; transfer to foil-lined baking sheet, skin side up. Bake 15 minutes or until cooked through (165°F).

3. To same skillet on medium, add shallots. Cook 2 minutes. Add white wine, dried rosemary, and ¼ teaspoon salt. Simmer 2 minutes, scraping up browned bits.

4. Whisk in sour cream and chicken broth.

5. Serve chicken with sauce; garnish with snipped chives.

SERVES 4: About 465 calories, 40g protein, 4g carbohydrates, 31g fat (9g saturated), 1g fiber, 615mg sodium.

> **TIP**
>
> The shallots add a distinctive flavor, but if you don't have any on hand you can use 1 small onion and a clove of garlic, and cook for 5 minutes.

Nashville Hot Chicken

If you've been to Nashville, you know hot chicken!
We tried it at Hattie B's, Bolton's, and Prince's Chicken,
then honed our own recipe so you can create it at home.

PREP: 25 MINUTES   TOTAL: 1 HOUR, PLUS BRINING

10 small pieces (3 pounds total) skin-on, bone-in chicken parts (if using breasts, cut in half)

5 cups water

¾ cup cayenne pepper hot sauce

2 tablespoons plus 2 teaspoons sugar

2¾ teaspoons granulated garlic

Salt

6 cups peanut oil

2 cups all-purpose flour

2 cups buttermilk

2 to 5 tablespoons cayenne pepper, to taste

2 teaspoons paprika

Ground black pepper

White bread and pickle slices, for serving

1. Place 1 gallon-size resealable plastic bag in a large bowl. Place the chicken in the bag.

2. In another bowl, whisk the water, hot sauce, 2 tablespoons sugar, 2 teaspoons garlic, and 3 tablespoons salt until the salt and sugar dissolve. Pour the mixture over the chicken; seal the bag. Refrigerate 5 to 8 hours.

3. Fit a wire rack into a foil-lined, rimmed baking sheet.

4. In a 12-inch-high, cast-iron skillet, heat the oil over medium-high heat until it registers 325°F on a deep-fry thermometer.

5. While the oil heats, place the flour in a large dish and the buttermilk in a large bowl. Drain chicken, discarding the brine. Dredge 5 pieces of chicken in the flour, then dip them in the buttermilk, letting the excess drip off. Dredge them in flour again, shaking off any excess. Carefully place each piece in the hot oil. Cook 12 to 18 minutes, or until chicken is deep golden brown and cooked through (165°F), turning it and adjusting the heat to maintain the oil temperature. Transfer the cooked chicken to the rack; sprinkle with ¼ teaspoon salt. Repeat with remaining chicken.

6. In another bowl, combine the cayenne to your taste, paprika, remaining 2 teaspoons sugar, remaining ¾ teaspoon garlic, and the black pepper to taste. Ladle ⅓ cup hot oil from the skillet into the bowl with the spices. Stir well.

7. To serve, brush the chicken generously with the spice paste and serve with white bread and pickle slices.

SERVES 5: About 725 calories, 43g protein, 43g carbohydrates, 42g fat (10g saturated), 3g fiber, 740mg sodium.

Buttermilk Fried Chicken

Don't be intimidated by the amount of hot sauce in this brine—
it adds a hint of heat and the acid helps infuse the chicken with
flavor. Longer marinating isn't better: Leaving the chicken in the
marinade overnight will actually toughen the proteins.

PREP: 25 MINUTES   TOTAL: 1 HOUR, PLUS BRINING

10 small pieces chicken (3 pounds), if using breasts cut in half

5 cups tepid water

¾ cup cayenne pepper hot sauce

2 tablespoons sugar

2 teaspoons garlic powder

Salt

4 cups canola oil

2 cups all-purpose flour

2 cups buttermilk

1. Place 1-gallon resealable plastic bag in large bowl. Add chicken to bag.

2. In another bowl, whisk water, hot sauce, sugar, garlic powder, and 3 tablespoons salt until salt dissolves. Pour over chicken in bag; seal bag. Refrigerate 3 to 5 hours.

3. Place wire rack over large, foil-lined rimmed baking sheet. In heavy, deep 12-inch skillet, heat oil on medium-high until 325°F on deep-fry thermometer.

4. While oil heats, place flour in large shallow dish and buttermilk in large bowl. Drain chicken and discard brine. Dredge 5 pieces in flour, then buttermilk, letting excess drip off, then return to flour again, shaking off excess. Place chicken in hot oil. Cook 12 to 18 minutes or until chicken is cooked through (165°F) and deep golden brown, turning occasionally and adjusting heat to maintain oil temperature.

5. Transfer cooked chicken to wire rack; sprinkle with ¼ teaspoon salt. Repeat breading and frying with remaining chicken. Serve with Corn-off-the-Cob Salad and drizzle of Hot Sauce Honey (recipes below).

SERVES 5: About 650 calories, 41g protein, 27g carbohydrates, 41g fat (7g saturated), 1g fiber, 650mg sodium.

Corn-off-the-Cob Salad

Whisk together **3 tablespoons lime juice**, **2 tablespoons Dijon mustard**, **½ teaspoon ground cumin**, **3 tablespoons olive oil**, and **½ teaspoon salt**. Cut kernels off **6 large corn ears**, grilled; add to dressing, along with **1 pint multicolored grape tomatoes**, halved, and **¼ cup each chopped cilantro and mint**. Stir until combined. Makes 6 cups.

Hot Sauce Honey

Microwave **¼ cup honey** on 50 percent power for 30 seconds or just until runny. Whisk in **2 tablespoons cayenne pepper hot sauce**. Makes about ⅓ cup.

Quick Chicken Mole

An easy weeknight riff on mole, made from pantry ingredients, this meal can be served with rice or warm tortillas. See photo on page 58.

See photo on page 58.

PREP: **15 MINUTES**   TOTAL: **40 MINUTES**

1 large onion, chopped

3 cloves garlic, chopped

2 teaspoons chili powder

1 tablespoon oil

1 cup salsa

1 cup chicken broth

½ cup Mixed-Nut Spread (recipe at right) or chocolate-hazelnut spread

2 pounds chicken parts, skin removed

Salt

Yellow rice, for serving

Sesame seeds and chopped green onions, for garnish

1. In 8-quart, heavy-bottomed pot on medium, cook onion, garlic, and chili powder in oil 7 minutes, stirring. Stir in salsa and chicken broth. Whisk in Mixed-Nut Spread.

2. Sprinkle chicken parts with ½ teaspoon salt; add to pot. Simmer 30 minutes or until chicken is cooked and tender. Serve with yellow rice. Garnish with sesame seeds and green onions.

SERVES 4: About 389 calories, 29g protein, 27g carbohydrates, 19g fat (5g saturated), 4g fiber, 1126mg sodium.

Mixed-Nut Spread

In food processor, process **¾ cup pecans**, **¼ cup unsalted cashews**, and **½ teaspoon salt** until mostly smooth and runny, about 8 minutes, stopping and scraping side of bowl occasionally. In medium bowl, melt **3½ ounces dark chocolate**, chopped, in microwave in 20-second intervals; stir in **1 cup sweetened condensed milk** and **2 tablespoons light corn syrup**. Add chocolate mixture to processed nuts; pulse until just combined. Makes about 2 cups. Store in airtight container at room temperature up to 2 weeks.

Crunchy Deviled Chicken

For the crispiest oven-fried chicken, nothing beats panko. Deviling usually involves mustard and a bit of spice. Here a hint of smoke comes from the paprika—irresistible and easy! See photo on page 6.

PREP: 15 MINUTES   TOTAL: 35 MINUTES

Nonstick cooking spray

3 tablespoons spicy brown mustard

1 large egg

½ teaspoon smoked paprika

1¼ pounds skinless, boneless chicken thighs

1¼ cups panko

1 pound medium carrots, halved lengthwise

Salt

Parsley, for garnish

Greens, for serving

1. Preheat oven to 450°F. Spray 2 rimmed baking sheets with nonstick cooking spray.

2. Whisk together spicy brown mustard, egg, and smoked paprika. Dip chicken thighs in egg mixture, then dredge through panko, pressing to adhere. Place on 1 prepared baking sheet.

3. On other sheet, arrange carrots. Spray chicken and carrots with nonstick cooking spray; sprinkle with ½ teaspoon salt. Bake for 20 minutes or until carrots are tender and chicken is cooked through (165°F). Garnish with parsley. Serve over greens.

SERVES 4: About 355 calories, 30g protein, 31g carbohydrates, 10g fat (3g saturated), 4g fiber, 605mg sodium.

TIP

Breading chicken is a cinch if you take a minute to arrange your steps: A shallow bowl or pie plate for the egg mixture and a large sheet of wax or parchment paper for the crumbs. Use one hand to dip chicken into the egg mixture; let excess egg drip off chicken then place onto the crumbs. Use your other hand to turn and coat the chicken. Lift paper up at edge to bring stray crumbs back to center.

Sheet Pan Chickpea Chicken

Sweet multicolor mini peppers need no trimming. If you don't find them in your market, core and seed 2 bell peppers and cut each into thin strips. Serve this dish with additional harissa if you like.

PREP: **5 MINUTES**   TOTAL: **35 MINUTES**

1 (15½-ounce) can chickpeas, rinsed

1 pound mini sweet peppers

2 tablespoons olive oil

Salt and ground black pepper

2 tablespoons harissa

4 small chicken legs

Fresh cilantro, for serving

1. Preheat oven to 425°F.

2. On large, rimmed baking sheet, place chickpeas. Toss with mini sweet peppers, 1 tablespoon olive oil, and ¼ teaspoon each salt and pepper.

3. In small bowl, whisk together harissa and 1 tablespoon olive oil. Rub sauce over the legs. Nestle among veggies; roast until chicken is cooked through (165°F), 20 to 25 minutes.

4. Top with fresh cilantro just before serving.

SERVES 4: About 630 calories, 39g protein, 22g carbohydrates, 42g fat (10g saturated), 6g fiber, 600mg sodium.

INGREDIENT IDEAS

Harissa is a North African spiced-chili paste. It usually includes garlic, caraway, coriander, cumin, and several types of dried chilies. It has lots of other possibilities:

- Marinate chicken wings (or other parts) in a few tablespoons.

- Add a teaspoon to salad dressing.

- Use straight up or stirred into mayo as a sandwich spread.

- Stir into Greek yogurt and use as a dressing for roasted veggies and grilled meat.

- Add a dollop to minestrone or bean soup

- Drizzle onto avocado toast and hummus.

Moroccan Chicken with Preserved Lemons & Olives

A common ingredient in North African cooking, preserved lemons are brined in lemon juice, salt, and water, and sometimes with additional spices. For this dish, you can substitute the grated zest of 1 lemon if you can't find the preserved ones in your market.

PREP: 25 MINUTES   TOTAL: 50 MINUTES

2 tablespoons olive oil

8 small chicken thighs (about 2¼ pounds total)

Kosher salt and ground black pepper

1 onion, thinly sliced

2 cloves garlic, finely chopped

1 teaspoon ground cumin

1 teaspoon ground cinnamon

½ teaspoon ground coriander

½ teaspoon ground ginger

1 cup low-sodium chicken broth

½ cup small pitted green olives

½ cup dried apricots, halved, or 3 fresh apricots, quartered (cut into wedges if large)

2 tablespoons chopped preserved lemon

¼ cup flat-leaf parsley, chopped

Sliced toasted almonds and couscous, for serving (optional)

1. Preheat oven to 425°F.

2. Heat oil in large oven-safe skillet on medium. Season chicken with ½ teaspoon each salt and pepper, and cook, skin side down, until golden brown and crisp, 10 minutes. Flip and cook 1 minute more; transfer to plate.

3. Place onion in skillet and cook, covered, stirring occasionally, until tender, 8 minutes. Uncover and stir in garlic, cumin, cinnamon, coriander, ginger, and ½ teaspoon each salt and pepper. Cook, stirring occasionally, until onion is golden brown, 5 to 6 minutes more.

4. Stir in broth, scraping up any browned bits. Return chicken (along with any juices) to skillet, along with olives, apricots, and preserved lemon. Transfer to oven and roast until chicken is cooked through (165°F), 8 to 10 minutes.

5. Sprinkle with parsley and almonds, and serve with couscous, if desired.

SERVES 4: About 605 calories, 38g protein, 10g carbohydrates, 45.5g fat (11g saturated), 3g fiber, 985mg sodium.

Quicker Coq au Vin Blanc

This French classic becomes easy enough for weeknight dinner with the help of an Instant Pot or electric pressure cooker.

PREP: 10 MINUTES   TOTAL: 35 MINUTES

4 ounces pancetta, chopped

2 teaspoons olive oil

3 pounds assorted chicken pieces

½ teaspoon dried thyme

Salt and ground black pepper

1 medium leek, thinly sliced

1½ cups dry white wine

1 pound golden potatoes, cut into 1-inch chunks

12 ounces cremini mushrooms, quartered

Chopped parsley, for garnish

TIP

You can use bacon if you don't have pancetta on hand. After cooking in Step 1, spoon out and discard all but 2 tablespoons fat.

1. In Instant Pot using sauté function, cook pancetta in oil 5 to 7 minutes or until fat has rendered. Transfer pancetta to paper towel–lined plate.

2. Meanwhile, pat chicken dry with paper towels; season all over with thyme and ½ teaspoon each salt and pepper.

3. In batches, add chicken, skin side down, to pot; cook 6 minutes or until browned on two sides, turning once halfway through. Transfer chicken to large plate.

4. To pot, add leek and ¼ teaspoon salt; cook 3 minutes, stirring. Add wine. Hit cancel, reselect sauté function, and adjust heat to More; heat to boiling. Hit cancel again, then reselect sauté function (this returns heat to Normal); simmer 5 minutes. Hit cancel to turn off sauté function.

5. Add potatoes, mushrooms, and chicken to pot. Cover and lock lid. Select Manual/Pressure Cook and cook at high pressure for 8 minutes. Once cooking is complete, release pressure by using a quick release.

6. Serve chicken and vegetables with some cooking liquid. Garnish with parsley.

SERVES 4: About 725 calories, 52g protein, 29g carbohydrates, 43g fat (13g saturated), 2g fiber, 785mg sodium.

Spicy Jerk Drumsticks

This dish is delicious for dinner, served with rice
and beans, or as game-time appetizer.

¼ cup olive oil

¼ cup soy sauce

3 tablespoons lime juice

3 tablespoons brown sugar

5 thin slices peeled fresh ginger

3 green onions, sliced

2 cloves garlic

3 jalapeño peppers or 1 habañero pepper

5 sprigs fresh thyme

¼ teaspoon ground allspice

Salt

12 chicken drumsticks

Sliced jalapeño peppers and lime wedges,
   for garnish

Coconutty Rice and Peas, for serving

1. In blender, puree oil, soy sauce, lime juice,
brown sugar, ginger, green onions, garlic,
chilies, thyme, allspice, and ¾ teaspoon salt
until smooth; transfer to gallon-size resealable
bag, along with chicken. Seal bag, removing
excess air. Toss to coat chicken; place bag on
large plate. Refrigerate at least 4 hours or up
to overnight.

2. Preheat oven to 425°F. Line large rimmed
baking sheet with foil; fit rack into baking sheet.

3. Remove drumsticks from marinade (discard
marinade) and gently pat dry with paper towels;
arrange on rack, spacing 1 inch apart. Roast 35
to 40 minutes or until cooked through (165°F).

4. Garnish with jalapeño peppers and lime
wedges, if desired. Serve with Coconutty Rice
& Peas.

SERVES 6: About 195 calories, 21g protein,
2g carbohydrates, 11g fat (3g saturated),
0g fiber, 300mg sodium.

Coconutty Rice & Peas

In large bowl or pot, combine **1 pound black-
eyed peas** and enough cold water to cover by
2 inches; cover and let stand overnight at room
temperature. Drain and rinse peas. In 6-quart
saucepot, heat **1 tablespoon vegetable oil** on
medium. Add **1 chopped medium onion** and
1 chopped carrot; cook 5 minutes, stirring
often. Add drained peas, **5 cups cold water and
3 bay leaves**. Partially cover; heat to boiling
on high. Reduce heat; simmer 30 to 35 minutes
or until peas are almost tender. Stir in **1 can
(14 ounces) coconut milk, 1 cup long grain
white rice**, and **1½ teaspoons salt**. Heat to
boiling on high. Cover and reduce heat; simmer
30 minutes. Remove from heat. Let stand
5 minutes. Discard bay leaves before serving.

Honey Mustard–Glazed Chicken Bake

A tangy sauce and fat drippings intensify the taste of roasted root vegetables, which act as the base for this chicken bake.

PREP: 30 MINUTES   TOTAL: 1 HOUR

1 pound parsnips, scrubbed and sliced on a bias

1 pound Yukon gold potatoes, scrubbed and quartered

½ pound carrots, peeled and sliced on a bias into 2-inch pieces

1 medium red onion, cut into 8 wedges

2 tablespoons olive oil

5 sprigs fresh thyme

Kosher salt

4 chicken thighs

4 chicken drumsticks

Ground black pepper

3 tablespoons Dijon mustard

2 tablespoons whole-grain mustard

2 tablespoons honey

1 tablespoon brown sugar

1. Preheat oven to 425°F.

2. On large baking sheet, toss parsnips, potatoes, carrots, onion, oil, thyme, and ½ teaspoon salt. Roast 15 minutes.

3. Remove baking sheet from oven. Season chicken with ½ teaspoon salt and ¼ teaspoon pepper, and arrange in single layer over vegetables. Return to oven and roast 15 minutes.

4. In medium bowl, whisk together Dijon mustard, whole-grain mustard, honey, and brown sugar. After 15 minutes, drizzle mustard mixture over chicken and vegetables and continue roasting until chicken is cooked through (165°F) and vegetables are tender, about 25 minutes.

SERVES 4: About 760 calories, 42g protein, 60g carbohydrates, 38g fat (9g saturated), 8g fiber, 995mg sodium.

Fennel Roasted Chicken & Peppers

Toasting the fennel and orange zest before grinding them into a spice blend deepen the flavors of this Provençal-style dish.

1½ teaspoons fennel seeds

1½ teaspoons finely grated orange zest

3 bell peppers (red, yellow, and orange), cut into 1-inch chunks

3 cloves garlic, thinly sliced

2 tablespoons olive oil

Kosher salt and ground black pepper

4 small chicken leg quarters (about 2 pounds)

4 cups baby spinach

2 ounces feta cheese, crumbled

1. Preheat oven to 425°F.

2. In small skillet, toast fennel seeds and orange zest until lightly browned and fragrant, 2 to 3 minutes. Transfer to mortar and pestle or spice grinder and crush or pulse to blend. Set aside.

3. On large rimmed baking sheet, toss bell peppers and garlic with 1 tablespoon oil and ½ teaspoon each salt and pepper.

4. Rub chicken legs with remaining tablespoon oil, then with fennel-orange mixture. Nestle among vegetables on baking sheet and roast until chicken is golden brown and cooked through, and peppers are tender, 25 to 30 minutes.

5. Transfer chicken to plates, scatter spinach over peppers remaining on baking sheet, and toss until just beginning to wilt. Sprinkle with feta and serve with chicken.

SERVES 4: About 500 calories, 32g protein, 11g carbohydrates, 37g fat (9g saturated), 3g fiber, 495mg sodium.

Skillet Pesto Chicken & Beans

The colors of the Italian flag unite in this yummy green
and white bean and tomato skillet bake.

PREP: **10 MINUTES**   TOTAL: **25 MINUTES**

8 small chicken thighs (about 2 pounds total)

Salt and ground black pepper

1 tablespoon olive oil

8 ounces green beans, halved

1 cup cherry tomatoes

1 (15-ounce) can butter beans, rinsed

2 tablespoons homemade or prepared pesto

Grated Parmesan and chopped basil,
   for serving

1. Preheat oven to 425°F.

2. Season chicken thighs with ½ teaspoon each
salt and pepper. Cook in olive oil on medium-
high, skin side down, in large oven-safe skillet
until golden brown, about 6 minutes.

3. Turn chicken over; add green beans, cherry
tomatoes, and butter beans, and season with
¼ teaspoon salt. Roast until chicken is cooked
through (165°F), 12 to 15 minutes.

4. Brush pesto over chicken and serve with
grated Parmesan and chopped basil.

SERVES 4: About 450 calories, 38g protein,
22g carbohydrates, 26g fat (6.5g saturated),
6g fiber, 770mg sodium.

Pesto

In a food processor or blender, pulse **3 cups
loosely packed fresh basil leaves, 1 large garlic
clove crushed with a press, ½ cup extra-virgin
olive oil, ¼ cup grated Parmesan cheese, ¼ cup
toasted pine nuts, 2 teaspoons fresh lemon
juice,** and ¼ **teaspoon ground black pepper**
until smooth. Scoop into a covered container
and refrigerate up to 3 days or freeze up to
3 months. Makes ¾ cup.

Grilled Chicken with White BBQ Sauce

Famous in Alabama, this creamy sauce will remind you
of ranch dressing—with a zip of horseradish.

PREP: **5 MINUTES**   TOTAL: **30 MINUTES**

4 pounds assorted chicken parts (thighs, drumsticks, wings)

Salt and ground black pepper

¾ cup White BBQ Sauce (recipe at right)

Parsley leaves, for garnish

1. Preheat grill to medium-low.

2. Season chicken all over with 1½ teaspoons salt and ½ teaspoon pepper. Grill chicken, covered, 20 minutes, turning occasionally.

3. Place White BBQ Sauce in bowl. Uncover chicken; generously brush with sauce. Turn chicken pieces over. Cook, brushing and turning chicken 2 more times, 5 minutes or until chicken is cooked through (165°F).

4. Garnish with parsley; serve with remaining sauce.

SERVES 8: About 375 calories, 29g protein, 1g carbohydrates, 28g fat (6g saturated), 0g fiber, 660mg sodium.

White BBQ Sauce

Whisk **1½ cups mayonnaise**; **¼ cup cider vinegar**; **2 tablespoons horseradish**, drained; **1 tablespoon lemon juice**; **¾ teaspoon sugar**; **¼ teaspoon cayenne (ground red) pepper**; **¾ teaspoon salt**; and **½ teaspoon black pepper** together, until smooth. Makes about 1¼ cups.

Mushroom Chicken Skillet with Herbed Cream Sauce

Vary the combination of mushrooms for this stovetop-to-oven skillet dish. If you like, you can swap in fresh tarragon for the thyme.

PREP: 20 MINUTES   TOTAL: 45 MINUTES

1 tablespoon butter

3 tablespoons olive oil

1 (10-ounce) package cremini mushrooms, sliced

8 ounces shiitake mushrooms, caps sliced

Kosher salt

1 large shallot, finely chopped

8 small chicken thighs (about 2¾ pounds total)

Ground black pepper

⅓ cup dry white wine

½ cup low-sodium chicken broth

3 sprigs thyme, plus more for garnish

1 tablespoon white miso

¼ cup heavy cream

1. Preheat oven to 375°F.

2. In large oven-safe skillet on medium-high, heat butter and 2 tablespoons oil. Once butter foams, add mushrooms and pinch salt, and cook, tossing occasionally, 5 minutes. Add shallots and cook, tossing occasionally, until mushrooms are golden brown, 2 to 3 minutes; transfer to plate and wipe skillet clean.

3. Return skillet to medium. Rub chicken with remaining 1 tablespoon oil and season with ¼ teaspoon each salt and pepper. Add chicken to skillet, skin side down, and cook until browned, 10 to 12 minutes; drain excess fat. Turn chicken over; add wine, then broth and thyme. Transfer skillet to oven and bake until chicken is cooked through (165°F), 5 to 6 minutes.

4. Transfer chicken to plate, discard thyme, and return skillet to medium heat. Whisk miso in skillet until dissolved, then simmer 3 minutes. Stir in cream and mushroom mixture and cook until heated through, about 2 minutes. Serve with chicken and additional thyme, if desired.

SERVES 4: About 620 calories, 46g protein, 11g carbohydrates, 44g fat (14g saturated), 2g fiber, 495mg sodium.

Spiced Sesame Chicken with Carrots & Couscous

If you want to use ground coriander and cumin instead of seeds in this Moroccan-inspired dish, decrease the amounts by one-third.

PREP: 10 MINUTES   TOTAL: 40 MINUTES

1 tablespoon coriander seeds, crushed

1 tablespoon sesame seeds

1 teaspoon cumin seeds, crushed

½ teaspoon coarsely cracked pepper

6 small to medium carrots, split lengthwise and cut into 2-inch pieces

2 tablespoons olive oil

Kosher salt

4 small chicken legs, split (4 thighs, 4 drumsticks)

1¼ cups couscous

2 tablespoons lime juice

2 green onions, thinly sliced

½ cups cilantro, chopped

1 teaspoon finely grated lime zest

1. Preheat oven to 450°F.

2. Mix together coriander seeds, sesame seeds, cumin seeds, and pepper.

3. On large rimmed baking sheet, toss carrots with 1 tablespoon oil and ¼ teaspoon salt. Rub chicken with ½ tablespoon oil and season with ½ teaspoon salt, then coat in spice mixture. Arrange chicken, skin side down, on same sheet and roast until chicken is cooked through and carrots are golden brown and tender, 28 to 30 minutes.

4. Meanwhile, cook couscous according to package directions. Fluff with fork, then toss with lime juice and remaining ½ tablespoon oil, and fold in green onions, cilantro, and lime zest.

5. Serve with chicken and carrots.

SERVES 4: About 675 calories, 55g protein, 53g carbohydrates, 26g fat (6g saturated), 6g fiber, 625mg sodium.

Sweet & Sticky Chicken with Snow Peas

Hoisin sauce is one of those pantry ingredients that adds rich flavor with no effort.

2½ pounds chicken drumsticks and thighs

¼ cup hoisin sauce

Salt and ground black pepper

1 pound snow peas

½ teaspoon crushed red pepper

2 teaspoons toasted sesame oil

Chopped cilantro, for garnish

1. Preheat oven to 450°F.

2. Toss chicken drumsticks and thighs with hoisin sauce and ½ teaspoon each salt and pepper. Arrange on foil-lined rimmed baking sheet. Roast 30 minutes or until cooked through (165°F).

3. Meanwhile, steam snow peas 3 minutes or until tender; drain and toss with crushed red pepper, toasted sesame oil, and pinch salt. Serve chicken over snow peas, garnished with chopped cilantro.

SERVES 4: About 370 calories, 38g protein, 16g carbohydrates, 16g fat (4g saturated), 4g fiber, 680mg sodium.

> **TIP**
>
> Having a party? Give wings the hoisin treatment in this recipe. For other wing flavors, see page 101.

ORANGE-GINGER ROAST CHICKEN
WITH FENNEL AND RADICCHIO
(PAGE 95)

3 | Cook It Whole

What's the easiest chicken prep of all? Roasting it whole, of course. A simple rub or glaze and a hands-off hour or so in the oven, and you've got dinner. For a ta-da dinner for friends, make the Orange-Ginger Roast Chicken with Fennel and Radicchio. Or start in the morning with this fix-it-and-forget-it Crock-Star Chicken with Walnut-Herb Sauce. This dish is ideal for a crowd. And sometimes you just want a better-than-rotisserie roast. Then it's time for Lemony Herb Roast Chicken—faster than a trip to the grocery store!

Roasted Jerk Chicken ················· 89

Garlic-Herb Cornish Hens············· 91

Apple & Thyme Roast Chicken·······92

Roast Chicken with 40 Cloves of Garlic···································93

Mahogany Roast Chicken·············94

Orange-Ginger Roast Chicken with Fennel and Radicchio ···········95

Lemony Herb Roast Chicken·········96

Crock-Star Chicken with Walnut-Herb Sauce ···················97

Roasted Jerk Chicken

This dish is party perfect. If you're not entertaining, save the second chicken for Spicy Bánh Mi Sandwiches (recipe below) or another of our recipes that calls for rotisserie chicken meat starting on page 112.

PREP: 15 MINUTES   **TOTAL:** 1 HOUR 30 MINUTES

4 green onions, sliced

3 cloves garlic

2 jalapeño peppers, sliced

¼ cup canola oil

3 tablespoons fresh lime juice

3 tablespoons soy sauce

2 tablespoons brown sugar

½ teaspoon ground allspice

1 teaspoon salt

½ teaspoon ground black pepper

2 whole chickens (about 4 pounds each)

1. Preheat the oven to 425°F. Line a large rimmed baking sheet with foil; place a rack on top of the foil.

2. In a blender, puree the green onions, garlic, jalapeño peppers, oil, lime juice, soy sauce, sugar, allspice, salt, and pepper until smooth.

3. Arrange the chickens on the rack. Gently loosen the chicken skin from the meat. Spoon some onion mixture into the cavity of the chicken and under the skin; rub the remaining mixture all over the exterior of the chicken. Tuck the wings behind the breast and tie the legs together with cooking twine. Roast 1 hour.

4. Reduce the oven temperature to 375°F. Roast another 15 minutes, or until the chicken is cooked through (165°F).

SERVES 8: About 600 calories, 60g protein, 5g carbohydrates, 36g fat (9g saturated), 0g fiber, 395mg sodium.

Spicy Bánh Mì Sandwiches

Thinly slice the **meat from 1 Roasted Jerk Chicken**; discard the skin and bones. Spread **1 cup mayonnaise** on **6 toasted sandwich rolls**. Top with the chicken, **1 thinly sliced cucumber**, **¾ cup shredded carrots**, and **½ cup fresh cilantro leaves**. Drizzle with **sriracha sauce**. Serves 6.

> **TIP**
>
> When carving, use a sharp, thin-bladed knife that is long enough to slice through the length of the breast.

Garlic-Herb Cornish Hens

If you can't find Cornish hens in your market, this spiced herb rub could be used on two four-pound chickens. See roasting instructions for Jerk Chicken (page 89).

PREP: 40 MINUTES   TOTAL: 1 HOUR 5 MINUTES, PLUS MARINATING

12 cloves garlic, peeled

¾ cup packed fresh mint leaves

¾ cup packed fresh basil leaves

½ cup red wine vinegar

⅓ cup soy sauce

½ cup packed fresh tarragon leaves

2 serrano chilies, stemmed and seeded

3 tablespoons sugar

1 tablespoon ground cumin

½ cup plus 3 tablespoons olive oil

Salt

4 large Cornish hens (about 1½ pounds each)

3 pounds baby new potatoes, cut into halves

Herb Sauce (recipe at right)

1. In a food processor or blender, puree the garlic, mint, basil, vinegar, soy sauce, tarragon, chilies, sugar, cumin, ½ cup oil, and 1½ teaspoons salt until smooth to create the marinade.

2. Place the hens in 2 gallon-size resealable plastic bags and add half the marinade to each. Seal the bags and turn them over a few times to distribute the marinade. Refrigerate at least overnight or up to 24 hours.

3. Preheat the oven to 425°F.

4. On a large rimmed baking sheet, arrange the hens, breast side up; discard the marinade. Tuck the wings behind the hens; tie the legs together with twine. Roast 45 minutes, or until the hens are cooked through (165°F). The hens are done when the temperature on a meat thermometer inserted in the thickest part of the thigh, next to the body but not touching bone, reaches the correct temperature and the juices run clear when the thigh is pierced with the tip of a knife. Let stand 10 minutes.

5. Meanwhile, on another large, rimmed baking sheet, toss the potatoes with the remaining 3 tablespoons oil and ¾ teaspoon salt. Roast 45 minutes, or until tender and browned, stirring once.

6. Using kitchen shears, cut each hen in half. Serve with potatoes and Herb Sauce.

SERVES 8 (each serving with ¼ cup sauce): About 755 calories, 41g protein, 35g carbohydrates, 49g fat (13g saturated), 3g fiber, 530mg sodium.

Herb Sauce

In a food processor, puree until smooth **1 cup sour cream**; **6 tablespoons fresh lime juice**; **¼ cup extra-virgin olive oil**; **½ cup fresh mint**; **½ cup fresh basil**; **2 tablespoons fresh tarragon**; **2 cloves peeled garlic**; **1 serrano chili**, stemmed and seeded; and **1 teaspoon salt**. Makes 2 cups.

Apple & Thyme Roast Chicken

This is a wonderful fall-is-in-the-air dinner. You can vary the apple variety, but choose one like Golden Delicious, Fuji, Rome, or Empire that will hold its shape when roasted.

PREP: 20 MINUTES   TOTAL: 1 HOUR 20 MINUTES

1 whole chicken (3½ pounds)

2 sprigs fresh thyme, plus 1 tablespoon chopped fresh thyme

¾ teaspoon salt

¼ teaspoon coarsely ground black pepper

⅛ teaspoon ground allspice

1 jumbo onion, cut into 12 wedges

¼ cup water

2 teaspoons olive oil

2 large Granny Smith apples, each cored and cut into quarters

2 tablespoons applejack brandy or calvados

½ cup chicken broth

1. Preheat the oven to 450°F.

2. Remove the giblets and neck from the chicken; reserve for another use. Pat chicken dry with paper towels.

3. With your fingertips, gently separate the skin from the meat on the chicken breast. Place 1 thyme sprig under the skin of each breast half. With the breast side up, lift the wings up toward the neck, then fold the wing tips under the back of the chicken so the wings stay in place. Tie the legs together with cooking twine.

4. In a cup, combine the chopped thyme, salt, pepper, and allspice.

5. In a medium-size roasting pan (14 × 10 inches), toss the onion with the thyme mixture, water, and oil. Push the onion mixture to the sides of the pan. Place the chicken, breast side up, on a small rack in the center of the roasting pan.

6. Roast the chicken and onion mixture for 40 minutes. Add the apples to the pan; roast about 20 minutes longer. The chicken is done when the temperature on a meat thermometer inserted in the thickest part of the thigh, next to the body but not touching bone, reaches 165°F and the juices run clear when the thigh is pierced with the tip of a knife. Transfer the chicken to a warm platter; let stand 10 minutes to set the juices for easier carving.

7. Meanwhile, remove the rack from the roasting pan. With a slotted spoon, transfer the onion mixture to the platter with the chicken. Skim the fat from the pan drippings and discard. Add the applejack to the pan drippings; cook 1 minute over medium heat, stirring constantly. Add the broth; heat to boiling. Serve the pan-juice mixture with the chicken; remove the skin from the chicken before eating, if desired.

SERVES 4 (each serving with skin): About 590 calories, 49g protein, 22g carbohydrates, 33g fat (9g saturated), 5g fiber, 708mg sodium.
SERVES 4 (each serving without skin): About 440 calories, 43g protein, 22g carbohydrates, 20g fat (5g saturated), 5g fiber, 686mg sodium.

Roast Chicken with 40 Cloves of Garlic

A great example of a recipe that is more than a sum of its ingredients. Roasting the garlic sweetens and softens it, and when mashed into the sauce the garlic adds richness and body.

PREP: 15 MINUTES   TOTAL: 1 HOUR 15 MINUTES

1 whole chicken (3½ pounds)

6 sprigs fresh thyme

½ teaspoon salt

¼ teaspoon coarsely ground black pepper

40 cloves garlic (from 2 heads), loose papery skin discarded but cloves unpeeled

1 cup chicken broth

Bread, for serving

1. Preheat the oven to 450°F.

2. Remove the giblets and neck from the chicken; reserve for another use. Pat the chicken dry with paper towels.

3. With your fingertips, gently separate the skin from the meat on the chicken breast. Place 2 thyme sprigs under the skin of each breast half. Place the remaining 2 sprigs inside the cavity of the chicken. Sprinkle salt and pepper on the outside of the chicken.

4. With the chicken breast side up, lift the wings up toward the neck, then fold the wing tips under the back of the chicken so the wings stay in place. Tie the legs together with cooking twine. Place the chicken, breast side up, on a rack in a small roasting pan (13 × 9 inches).

5. Roast the chicken 30 minutes. Add the garlic to the bottom of the pan around the chicken; roast about 30 minutes longer. The chicken is done when the temperature on a meat

thermometer inserted in the thickest part of the thigh, next to the body but not touching bone, reaches 165°F and the juices run clear when the thigh is pierced with the tip of a knife.

6. Transfer the chicken to a warm platter; let stand 10 minutes to set the juices for easier carving.

7. Meanwhile, remove the rack from the roasting pan. With a slotted spoon, transfer the garlic cloves to a small bowl. Skim and discard the fat from the pan drippings. Remove and discard the skin from 6 garlic cloves; return the peeled garlic to the roasting pan and add broth. Heat the broth mixture to boiling over medium heat, stirring to loosen the browned bits from the bottom of the pan and mashing the garlic with the back of a spoon until well blended.

8. Serve the chicken with pan juices, remaining garlic cloves, and bread. Remove the skin from the chicken before eating, if desired.

SERVES 4 (each serving with skin): About 500 calories, 50g protein, 11g carbohydrates, 28g fat (8g saturated), 1g fiber, 688mg sodium.
SERVES 4 (each serving without skin): About 355 calories, 44g protein, 10g carbohydrates, 14g fat (4g saturated), 1g fiber, 667mg sodium.

Mahogany Roast Chicken

The repeated glazing of the chicken during roasting adds
to its characteristic color. If you don't have vermouth in
your liquor cabinet, you can use red or white wine.

PREP: 10 MINUTES   TOTAL: 1 HOUR 25 MINUTES

1 whole chicken (3½ pounds)

¾ teaspoon salt

½ teaspoon coarsely ground black pepper

2 tablespoons dark brown sugar

2 tablespoons balsamic vinegar

2 tablespoons dry vermouth

¼ cup water

1. Preheat the oven to 375°F.

2. Remove the giblets and neck from the chicken; reserve for another use. Pat dry with paper towels. Sprinkle salt and pepper on the outside of the chicken.

3. With the chicken breast side up, lift the wings up toward neck, then fold the wing tips under the back of the chicken so the wings stay in place. Tie the legs together with cooking twine. Place the chicken, breast side up, on a rack in a small roasting pan (13 × 9 inches). Roast the chicken 45 minutes.

4. Meanwhile, prepare the glaze: In a bowl, stir together the brown sugar, vinegar, and vermouth until the sugar dissolves.

5. After the chicken has roasted 45 minutes, brush it with some of the glaze. Turn the oven temperature up to 400°F and continue to roast the chicken, glazing twice more, until the chicken is deep brown, about 30 minutes longer. The chicken is done when the temperature on a meat thermometer inserted into the thickest part of the thigh, next to the body but not touching bone, reaches 165°F and the juices run clear when the thigh is pierced with the tip of a knife.

6. Transfer the chicken to a warm platter; let stand 10 minutes to set the juices for easier carving.

7. Meanwhile, add ¼ cup water to roasting pan; over medium heat, heat to boiling, stirring to loosen brown bits. Remove pan from heat; skim and discard fat.

8. Serve the chicken with the pan juices.

SERVES 4: About 445 calories, 48g protein, 7g carbohydrates, 24g fat (7g saturated), 0g fiber, 583mg sodium.

TIP

Letting the bird rest after roasting results in firmer, juicer meat that is easier to carve. Poultry should stand at least 10 minutes before carving so the juices can relax back into the meat.

Orange-Ginger Roast Chicken with Fennel and Radicchio

Toss sweet roasted fennel and mushrooms with bitter radicchio for a delicious side to this gingery bird. See photo on page 86.

See photo on page 86.

PREP: 10 MINUTES   TOTAL: 1 HOUR 30 MINUTES

2 bulbs fennel, cored and sliced into ¼-inch pieces

1 tablespoon olive oil

Kosher salt and ground black pepper

1 navel orange

2 tablespoons honey

2 tablespoons grated fresh ginger

2 teaspoons fennel seeds, coarsely crushed

1 (4- to 5-pound) chicken, giblets discarded or reserved for another use

1 pound mixed mushrooms, cut if large

1 tablespoon sherry vinegar

1 small head radicchio, torn into large pieces

Chopped flat-leaf parsley, for serving (optional)

1. Preheat oven to 350°F.

2. Line rimmed baking sheet with parchment paper. On prepared sheet, toss fennel with oil and ½ teaspoon each salt and pepper. Move to outer edges of pan.

3. Grate zest of orange into small bowl, then squeeze in 3 tablespoons juice (reserve orange halves). Whisk in honey to dissolve, then stir in ginger and fennel seeds.

4. Pat chicken dry and place in center of prepared baking sheet. Stuff with orange halves, then brush with half of juice mixture. Roast 40 minutes.

5. Increase oven temperature to 425°F. Toss mushrooms with fennel and brush chicken with remaining juice mixture. Roast until temperature reaches 165°F on meat thermometer inserted into thickest part of thigh, 25 to 30 minutes. Transfer chicken to cutting board and let rest at least 10 minutes before carving.

6. Toss mushrooms and fennel mixture with vinegar, season with salt and pepper if necessary, and then fold in radicchio. Serve with chicken, topped with parsley, if desired.

SERVES 8: About 345 calories, 32g protein, 13g carbohydrates, 18.5g fat (5g saturated), 3g fiber, 245mg sodium.

Lemony Herb Roast Chicken

Roasting radishes brings out a sweetness you may not know they have. Mixed into this bread salad, radishes are also a sensational complement to the lemony chicken.

PREP: 15 MINUTES   TOTAL: 1 HOUR 20 MINUTES

2 teaspoons finely grated lemon zest

2 cloves garlic, crushed with press

1 teaspoon fresh thyme, chopped

4 tablespoons butter, softened

Salt and ground black pepper

1 whole chicken (4 to 5 pounds), patted dry

1 medium onion, thinly sliced

1 bunch radishes, trimmed, quartered

Radish & Fennel Panzanella (recipe at right)

1. Preheat oven to 350°F.

2. In bowl, mash zest, garlic, thyme, 2 tablespoons butter, and ½ teaspoon each salt and pepper until combined. With fingers, gently separate skin from breast and thighs of chicken. Place butter mixture under skin; spread evenly. Tie drumsticks together and tuck wings behind breast.

3. Place chicken on rack fitted into medium-size roasting pan. Arrange onion and radishes around chicken. Melt remaining 2 tablespoons butter; brush all over chicken, then sprinkle with ½ teaspoon each salt and pepper. Pour ¼ cup water into bottom of roasting pan.

4. Roast chicken 50 minutes. Increase oven temperature to 425°F; roast, checking to make sure water has not completely evaporated (add another ¼ cup if necessary), 15 to 20 minutes or until meat thermometer inserted into thickest part of thigh registers 165°F.

5. Let chicken rest at least 15 minutes before carving.

6. Meanwhile, use roasted onions and radishes and any pan juices to prepare Radish & Fennel Panzanella.

SERVES 6 (chicken only): About 415 calories, 40g protein, 1g carbohydrates, 27g fat (10g saturated), 0g fiber, 345mg sodium.

Radish & Fennel Panzanella

On large cookie sheet, toast **4 cups torn crusty bread** in 425°F oven, 6 to 10 minutes or until golden brown and crisp; let cool. In large bowl, whisk **¼ cup lemon juice**, **2 tablespoons Dijon mustard**, and **¼ teaspoon each salt and pepper** until smooth. When ready to serve, add **1 medium bulb fennel**, trimmed, cored and thinly sliced; **4 cups arugula**; **toasted bread**; and **roasted onions and radishes** to bowl; toss well.

Crock-Star Chicken with Walnut-Herb Sauce

We crave this chicken dish with its warm spices and cool cabbage-kohlrabi slaw. Leftovers, if there are any, make delicious sandwiches. See photo on page 8.

PREP: 40 MINUTES   TOTAL: 4 HOURS 40 MINUTES

1 medium onion, cut into ½-inch slices

2 tablespoons olive oil

1 tablespoon ground coriander

¼ teaspoon ground cinnamon

Ground black pepper

1 whole chicken (about 4 pounds)

Salt

⅔ cup walnuts, toasted

½ cup packed fresh mint leaves, plus more for garnish

¼ cup packed fresh basil leaves

1 tablespoon lemon juice

6 flatbreads, toasted

Cabbage-Kohlrabi Slaw (recipe at right)

1. Arrange onion in single layer toward center of bottom of 6- to 8-quart slow-cooker bowl. Combine oil, coriander, cinnamon, and ½ teaspoon pepper; rub all over and inside chicken. With cooking twine, tie drumsticks together. Sprinkle all over with ¾ teaspoon salt. Place chicken on onion in slow-cooker bowl.

2. Cover and cook on high 4 hours. Transfer chicken to cutting board.

3. In blender, puree 1 cup liquid from slow cooker with onion, walnuts, mint, basil, lemon juice, and ¼ teaspoon salt until smooth.

4. Serve chicken with walnut-herb sauce, flatbreads, and Cabbage-Kohlrabi Slaw.

SERVES 6: About 785 calories, 45g protein, 54g carbohydrates, 44g fat (11g saturated), 7g fiber, 1,005mg sodium.

Cabbage-Kohlrabi Slaw

Toss together **4 cups thinly sliced red cabbage**; **2 small bulbs kohlrabi (or 1 large bulb jicama)**, peeled and cut into matchsticks; **1 seedless (English) cucumber**, center removed, cut into matchsticks; **½ cup loosely packed fresh parsley**; **2 green onions**, thinly sliced on an angle; **¼ cup lemon juice**; and **¼ teaspoon salt**.

BBQ CHICKEN & CHEDDAR
BURGERS (PAGE 103)

4 Wings & Ground Chicken

Our answer to wings is always YES! Whether you want Fiery Buffalo or Sweet 'n' Sticky Thai or Ballpark-inspired, our oven-roasting method delivers crisp, tasty wings without the spattering mess. For a crowd, you can double the recipe using two pans. Be sure to rotate pans, from top to bottom racks, halfway through roasting. Plus, we love ground chicken for its delicious, lighter flavor, compared to other ground meats. Whether your sear it, poach it, or stir-fry it, chicken can take on flavors from BBQ to feta and mint. Check out our Lemon-Dill Chicken Meatball Soup, Loaded Chicken Burgers, Mustard-Crusted Mini Meat Loaves with Roasted Apples, and Thai Basil Stir-Fry.

Wings of Desire·····················101
Loaded Chicken Burgers·············102
BBQ Chicken & Cheddar Burgers ··103
Thai Basil Stir-Fry ·····················105
Mustard-Crusted Mini Meat Loaves with Roasted Apples········106
Feta & Mint Mini Meat Loaves·······107
Lemon-Dill Chicken Meatball Soup ·····················109

BOURBON BARBECUE SAUCE

SWEET 'N' STICKY THAI WINGS

HOT CARIBBEAN WINGS

BUFFALO WINGS

SESAME TERIYAKI SAUCE

Wings of Desire

They're baked, but these crispy-charred wings rival fried, thanks
to the six knockout sauces here. Just pick your favorite.

PREP: 10 MINUTES   TOTAL: 45 MINUTES

2½ pounds split chicken wings
Salt

1. Preheat oven to 425°F.

2. Pierce chicken wings all over with tip of knife;
pat dry. Place on wire rack fitted into large,
foil-lined jelly-roll pan. Sprinkle with ⅛ teaspoon
salt.

3. Bake 35 minutes or until cooked through
(165°F), turning over once.

4. Preheat broiler. Broil wings 7 minutes on high,
turning once. Toss with desired sauce; makes
about 25 wings.

SERVES 6 (chicken only): About 225 calories,
21g protein, 0g carbohydrates, 15g fat (4g saturated),
0g fiber, 127mg sodium.

FUN FLAVORS

Sweet 'n' Sticky Thai Wings

In bowl, stir **½ cup Thai sweet chili sauce**, zest of
1 lime, and **1 teaspoon fish sauce**; toss with cooked
wings and **⅓ cup french-fried onions**.

Hot Caribbean Wings

In 2-quart saucepan, mix **1 cup mango nectar**,
2 teaspoons habañero hot sauce, a **pinch of allspice**,
and **⅛ teaspoon each salt and black pepper**. Cook
on medium-high 8 minutes to reduce by half. Stir in
2 teaspoons lime juice; toss with cooked wings and
¼ cup chopped cilantro.

Bourbon BBQ Wings

In 2-quart saucepan, combine **¾ cup barbecue sauce**,
¼ cup bourbon, and **1 tablespoon yellow mustard**.
Heat to simmering on medium-high; simmer 3 minutes,
stirring. Transfer to bowl; toss with cooked wings.

Sesame Teriyaki Wings

In large bowl, whisk together **3 tablespoons teriyaki
sauce**, **2 tablespoons rice vinegar**, **1 tablespoon dark
brown sugar**, and **2 teaspoons toasted sesame oil**; toss
with cooked wings and **2 tablespoons sesame seeds**.

Fiery Buffalo Wings

In 1-quart saucepan, melt **2 tablespoons butter** on
medium. Whisk in **½ cup hot sauce** and **2 tablespoons
distilled white vinegar**. Transfer to bowl; toss with
cooked wings and **¼ cup blue cheese dip**.

Loaded Chicken Burgers

We love the crunch the potato chips add to this all-in burger.
If you like, use plain or dill pickle–flavored chips instead.

PREP: 5 MINUTES   **TOTAL: 20 MINUTES**

1 pound ground dark-meat chicken

3 tablespoons Italian-style bread crumbs

¼ cup Parmesan, grated

1 large egg

Salt and ground black pepper

2 teaspoons vegetable oil

Toasted buns, for serving

**Lettuce, tomato, ketchup, mustard, and 2 cups
  barbecue-flavored potato chips, for topping**

1. Combine ground chicken, bread crumbs, Parmesan, egg, ¼ teaspoon salt, and ½ teaspoon pepper. Form into four 1-inch-thick patties.

2. In 12-inch nonstick skillet, heat vegetable oil on medium. Add patties; cook 8 to 10 minutes or until cooked through (165°F), turning once.

3. Serve on toasted buns, topped with lettuce, tomato, ketchup, mustard, and potato chips.

SERVES 4: About 470 calories, 33g protein, 42g carbohydrates, 19g fat (5g saturated), 2g fiber, 960mg sodium.

TIP

For juicy tender burgers, don't overmix the meat with the other ingredients. When shaping burgers use a gentle touch—don't squeeze or compress the mixture. To ensure even cooking, make a thumbprint in the center of each burger. The centers tend to puff up during cooking and this will keep it even.

BBQ Chicken & Cheddar Burgers

Barbecue sauce does double duty, adding flavor and moisture to these All-American burgers. Plus, we love the crisp tartness of the green apple with the cheddar. See photo on page 98.

See photo on page 98.

PREP: 10 MINUTES   TOTAL: 25 MINUTES

1¼ pounds ground chicken

⅓ cup barbecue sauce

3 green onions, chopped

Salt and pepper

2 teaspoons canola oil

4 slices sharp Cheddar cheese

4 whole-wheat buns

Thinly sliced green apple and microgreens, as topping

1. Combine ground chicken, barbecue sauce, green onions, and ¼ teaspoon each salt and pepper. Form into four 1-inch-thick patties.

2. In 12-inch nonstick skillet, heat canola oil on medium; add patties. Cook 7 minutes per side or until cooked through (165°F). Top each patty with 1 slice sharp Cheddar cheese; remove from heat and cover skillet to melt cheese.

3. Serve on whole-wheat buns, topped with thinly sliced green apple and microgreens.

SERVES 4: About 475 calories, 36g protein, 35g carbohydrates, 23g fat (8g saturated), 5g fiber, 795mg sodium.

TIP

If you want to make your own ground chicken, chop up 1½ pounds breast and thigh meat; freeze the chunks just until firm. Add the chicken to a food processor and pulse until finely chopped but not pasty.

Thai Basil Stir-Fry

You can chop your own chicken in the food processor
(see tip page 103), for a more traditional dish.

1 medium onion, finely chopped

4 cloves garlic, chopped

2 tablespoons canola oil

1 pound ground chicken

3 tablespoons fish sauce

½ cup packed fresh basil leaves

2 tablespoons lime juice

Steamed rice, for serving

1 cup shredded carrots and additional basil,
   for topping

1. In 12-inch skillet on medium, cook onion and garlic in canola oil 6 minutes or until garlic is golden, stirring occasionally. Add ground chicken.

2. Increase heat to medium-high. Cook 5 minutes or until browned, stirring occasionally.

3. Add fish sauce; cook 1 minute. Remove from heat; stir in basil leaves and lime juice.

4. Serve over steamed rice, topped with shredded carrots and additional basil.

SERVES 4: About 256 calories, 22g protein,
7g carbohydrates, 16g fat (3g saturated),
1g fiber, 973mg sodium.

TIP

Fish sauce—a seasoning made from fermented fish, often anchovies—is an integral part of the cooking of Vietnam (where it is called Nuoc nam) and Thailand (nam pla). It adds a salty, briny flavor to dishes. Store it in a cool dark place for up to a year.

Mustard-Crusted Mini Meat Loaves with Roasted Apples

Shredded zucchini adds moisture to these savory meat loaves.
You can swap in thyme for the rosemary if you prefer.

PREP: 15 MINUTES   TOTAL: 45 MINUTES

1¼ pounds ground chicken

1 small zucchini, grated

⅓ cup seasoned bread crumbs

Salt and ground black pepper

2 tablespoons Dijon mustard

3 small Gala or Empire apples, cored and cut into 8 wedges

1 teaspoon fresh rosemary, chopped

¼ teaspoon cayenne (ground red) pepper

1 tablespoon olive oil

Snipped chives, for garnish

1. Preheat oven to 425°F.

2. In large bowl, combine ground chicken, zucchini, seasoned bread crumbs, and ½ teaspoon each salt and pepper. Form into 4 loaves. Place on foil-lined, rimmed baking sheet; brush with Dijon mustard.

3. Toss apples with rosemary, cayenne pepper, olive oil, and pinch salt; arrange around meat loaves. Bake 30 minutes or until loaves are cooked through (165°F).

4. Garnish with snipped chives.

SERVES 4: About 391 calories, 32g protein, 25g carbohydrates, 19g fat (5g saturated), 4g fiber, 677mg sodium.

Feta & Mint Mini Meat Loaves

You can also serve these meat loaves with a simple
Greek salad of tomatoes, cucumbers, and feta.

PREP: 10 MINUTES   TOTAL: 30 MINUTES

1¼ pounds ground chicken

½ cup crumbled feta cheese

½ cup fresh mint, finely chopped

Salt

1 large leek, well rinsed and sliced

3 medium yellow squash, chopped

1 cup pitted green olives

1 tablespoon olive oil

1. Preheat the oven to 450°F.

2. Combine the ground chicken, feta, mint, and ¼ teaspoon salt. Form into 4 mini loaves on a baking sheet.

3. Toss the leek, squash, and olives with the olive oil and ⅛ teaspoon salt; arrange the mixture around the loaves on the baking sheet. Roast 15 to 20 minutes, or until the meat loaves are cooked through (165°F).

SERVES 4: About 413 calories, 35g protein, 12g carbohydrates, 27g fat (8g saturated), 4g fiber, 965mg sodium.

TIP

Dark-colored pans hold more heat and brown foods more quickly. If you're roasting meat or veggies, the darker finish helps your roasting! If you're baking cookies, go light—even if you choose a baking sheet with a nonstick finish.

Lemon-Dill Chicken Meatball Soup

Springtime in a bowl! Bulgur and meatballs make
this citrus-enhanced soup a one-pot meal.

PREP: 15 MINUTES   TOTAL: 40 MINUTES

2 carrots, sliced

2 stalks celery, sliced

1 small onion, chopped

2 tablespoons olive oil

5 cups low-sodium chicken broth

3 cups water

1¾ cups bulgur

12 ounces ground chicken breast

¼ cup fresh dill, finely chopped

1 teaspoon lemon zest, grated

Salt and ground black pepper

1. In 6- to 7-quart saucepot on medium, cook carrots, celery, and onion in olive oil, 10 minutes, stirring. Add chicken broth and water; heat to boiling on high. Stir in bulgur. Reduce heat; simmer 8 to 10 minutes or until bulgur is almost tender.

2. Meanwhile, combine ground chicken breast, dill, lemon zest, and ¼ teaspoon each salt and pepper. Form chicken mixture into 1-inch balls; add to simmering soup along with ¼ teaspoon salt. Cook 6 minutes or until cooked through (165°F).

SERVES 4: About 435 calories, 22g protein, 53g carbohydrates, 16g fat (1g saturated), 9g fiber, 925mg sodium.

TIP

Want this soup even faster? Omit step 2. Instead of the meatballs, shred enough rotisserie chicken to equal 2 cups. Add chicken along with the dill, lemon zest, salt, and pepper to the soup and cook just until chicken is heated through.

ENCHILADAS VERDES
(PAGE 116)

5 | Rotisserie Chicken Meals

Rotisserie chicken's status has gone from a grab-and-go dinner to a tasty go-to base for salads, soups, sandwiches, and pizzas. Try it tossed with pesto in our Pesto Chicken Salad Croissants, spiked with homemade green sauce in Enchiladas Verdes, or drizzled with vinaigrette in Rotisserie Chicken Cobb salad or Reina Pepiada (chicken-and-avocado sandwiches). Plus, there are Broccoli-Parmesan Chicken Soup, Buffalo Chicken Baguette Pizza, and more to tempt you. If you can, use rotisserie chicken within a day of purchase—it's at its prime texture and flavor on the day it's roasted.

Buffalo Chicken Baguette Pizza···· 112

Reina Pepiada ························· 113

Chicken Taco Pizzas ················· 115

Enchiladas Verdes ···················· 116

Pesto Chicken Salad Croissants ···· 117

Rotisserie Chicken Cobb············· 119

Broccoli-Parmesan Chicken Soup ····································· 121

Finger-Lickin' Biscuit Loaf···········123

Buffalo Chicken Baguette Pizza

We have a weakness for anything Buffalo, and this pizza wins for deliciousness and ease. Serve it as a party appetizer or for dinner with a salad, with some celery in it, of course!

PREP: 10 MINUTES   TOTAL: 25 MINUTES

1 (24-inch) baguette

2 cups shredded rotisserie chicken

⅔ cup Buffalo-style hot sauce

¼ cup ranch dressing, plus more for topping

6 ounces mozzarella, coarsely grated

½ cup crumbled blue cheese

2 green onions, thinly sliced

Chopped cilantro, for topping

1. Place an oven rack in middle of oven and preheat broiler.

2. Split baguette lengthwise and arrange on baking sheet, cut side up. Broil until light golden brown, 2 to 3 minutes. Remove from oven.

3. Reduce oven temperature to 375°F.

4. Meanwhile, in small bowl, combine chicken and hot sauce; set aside.

5. Spread 2 tablespoons ranch dressing over cut side of bread and sprinkle with mozzarella. Top with chicken mixture and blue cheese.

6. Bake until cheese has melted, and bread is crisp, 3 to 5 minutes. Top with green onions and cilantro, and drizzle with additional ranch, if desired.

SERVES 6: About 450 calories, 26g protein, 48g carbohydrates, 20g fat (8g saturated), 3g fiber, 1,705mg sodium.

Reina Pepiada

We loves these Venezuelan chicken-and-avocado sandwiches; the warm corn cakes have a more delicate flavor than corn tortillas and a pillowy texture. That said, if you can't find masarepa to make the arepas, you could use warmed corn tortillas instead.

TOTAL: 15 MINUTES

2 ripe avocados

3 tablespoons mayonnaise

2 tablespoons fresh lime juice

Kosher salt

2 cups shredded rotisserie chicken

2 green onions, finely chopped

½ jalapeño pepper, seeded and finely chopped

¼ cup cilantro, finely chopped

Venezuelan Arepas (recipe at right)

1. In bowl, mash avocado (about 2 cups) with mayonnaise, lime juice, and ½ teaspoon salt.

2. Add chicken and gently toss to coat. Then fold in green onions, jalapeño pepper, and cilantro.

3. Fill Venezuelan Arepas with chicken salad.

SERVES 8 (salad only): About 165 calories, 7g protein, 6g carbohydrates, 16g fat (3g saturated), 4g fiber, 300mg sodium.

Venezuelan Arepas

In large bowl, combine **2 cups precooked cornmeal** (masarepa, not masa harina) and **2 teaspoons salt**. Add **2½ cups warm water** and whisk to remove lumps, then stir with spatula to combine. Let rest 5 minutes. Divide dough into 8 balls and flatten each into a 3-inch disk about ½ inch thick. Heat **1 tablespoon canola oil** in large nonstick skillet on medium. In 2 batches, cook 4 arepas, covered, until golden brown on one side, 6 to 8 minutes. Uncover, flip, and cook until other side is golden brown, 5 to 7 minutes more. Transfer to wire rack and repeat with remaining **1 tablespoon oil** and arepas. Split and stuff with Reina Pepiada.

Chicken Taco Pizzas

Look for thick, gyro-style pitas or flatbreads to hold all the garnishes.

PREP: 15 MINUTES   TOTAL: 25 MINUTES

4 (6-inch) flatbreads or pitas

Nonstick cooking spray

2 cups pulled rotisserie chicken meat

1 chipotle chili in adobo, finely chopped

1 teaspoon ground cumin

½ teaspoon garlic powder

½ cup sour cream

½ cup pickled, mild jalapeño peppers, drained and sliced

1 cup shredded sharp Cheddar

Shredded lettuce and fresh cilantro, for garnish

1. Preheat oven to 450°F.

2. Arrange flatbreads or pitas on large, foil-lined baking sheet. Spray bread with nonstick cooking spray. Stir together chicken meat, chili, cumin, and garlic powder. Divide evenly among breads.

3. Drizzle chicken with sour cream. Top with jalapeño peppers and shredded sharp Cheddar. Bake 10 to 12 minutes or until bottom is golden brown.

4. Garnish with shredded lettuce and fresh cilantro.

SERVES 4: About 440 calories, 24g protein, 39g carbohydrates, 24g fat (11g saturated), 2g fiber, 995mg sodium.

Enchiladas Verdes

Homemade salsa verde is delicious and easy to make. Be sure to let the vegetables char a bit to get traditional smoky flavor. See photo on page 110.

PREP: 20 MINUTES   TOTAL: 40 MINUTES

10 ounces tomatillos (about 4), halved

2 cloves unpeeled garlic

1 large yellow onion, cut into 1-inch-thick wedges

1 large poblano pepper, halved and seeded

1 jalapeño pepper, halved and seeded

1 tablespoon olive oil

Kosher salt and pepper

1½ cups cilantro leaves, plus additional ½ cup coarsely chopped cilantro

7 tablespoons fresh lime juice

3 cups shredded rotisserie chicken

2 green onions, thinly sliced

1½ cups shredded Monterey Jack cheese

½ cup salsa verde

8 small corn tortillas

1 small red onion, thinly sliced (optional)

Cilantro, for topping (optional)

1. Preheat broiler.

2. On large, rimmed baking sheet, toss tomatillos, garlic, onions, poblanos, and jalapeño peppers with oil and ½ teaspoon each salt and pepper. Turn peppers cut side down and broil, rotating pan every 5 minutes until vegetables are tender and charred, 15 minutes. Discard skins from poblanos and garlic. Transfer broiled vegetables to blender. Add 1½ cups cilantro leaves, 3 tablespoons fresh lime juice, and ¼ teaspoon salt and puree until smooth.

3. Preheat oven to 400°F. In bowl, toss chicken with green onions and 2 tablespoons fresh lime juice. Fold in ½ cup chopped cilantro and 1 cup shredded Monterey Jack cheese.

4. Spread ½ cup salsa verde in 13 × 9-inch baking dish and transfer rest to bowl. Dip each of the tortillas in salsa, then fill each with about ½ cup chicken mixture. Roll tortillas around filling and place, seam side down, in prepared dish. Top with any remaining salsa and sprinkle with ½ cup shredded Monterey Jack. Bake until beginning to brown, 8 to 10 minutes.

5. Meanwhile, toss red onion with 2 tablespoons fresh lime juice and pinch each salt and pepper; let sit 10 minutes. Top enchiladas with pickled onions and cilantro, if desired.

SERVES 4: About 500 calories, 30g protein, 39g carbohydrates, 32g fat (11g saturated), 6g fiber, 1,215mg sodium.

Pesto Chicken Salad Croissants

This is the ideal picnic food! For a party, look for mini croissants—they're easy to handle. You'll find them bagged in the bakery section of the grocery store.

PREP: 15 MINUTES   TOTAL: 20 MINUTES

½ cup plain yogurt

¼ cup pesto

2 teaspoons lemon zest, plus 1 tablespoon juice

Kosher salt and ground black pepper

3 cups shredded rotisserie chicken

⅓ cup sliced toasted almonds

6 croissants, split and toasted

Baby arugula and sprouts, for serving

1. In large bowl, whisk together yogurt, pesto, lemon zest and juice, and ¼ teaspoon each salt and pepper. Fold in chicken and almonds.

2. Place chicken salad in croissants, dividing chicken salad and arugula among croissants; top with sprouts.

SERVES 6: About 435 calories, 20g protein, 31g carbohydrates, 30g fat (10.5g saturated), 3g fiber, 705mg sodium.

Easy Chicken Salad

In a large bowl, combine **3 stalks finely chopped celery**, **⅓ cup mayonnaise**, **2 teaspoons fresh lemon juice**, **½ teaspoon salt**, and **¼ teaspoons ground black pepper**; stir until blended. Add **2 cups chopped rotisserie chicken** and toss to coat.

BASIL & SUN-DRIED TOMATO CHICKEN SALAD

Prepare as directed but add **¼ cup chopped fresh basil** and **2 tablespoons finely chopped oil-packed sun-dried tomatoes**, drained, to the mayonnaise mixture.

CURRY-GRAPE CHICKEN SALAD

Prepare as directed, but add **2 cups red or green seedless grapes**, cut in half; **1 teaspoon curry powder**; and **1 teaspoon honey** to the mayonnaise mixture.

LEMON-PEPPER CHICKEN SALAD

Prepare as directed but use **1 tablespoon fresh lemon juice** and **½ teaspoon coarsely ground black pepper**; add **½ teaspoon freshly grated lemon zest** to the mayonnaise mixture.

Rotisserie Chicken Cobb

Toss these Cobb salad ingredients for a casual meal that comes together in no time. If you want an added special touch, go ahead and arrange each ingredient in rows over the lettuce, then drizzle with the vinaigrette. Yum!

PREP: 15 MINUTES   TOTAL: 20 MINUTES

2 tablespoons extra-virgin olive oil

2 tablespoons red wine vinegar

Salt and ground black pepper

2 plum tomatoes, diced

3 cups shredded rotisserie chicken meat

1 avocado, diced

4 slices cooked bacon, broken into pieces

¼ cup crumbled blue cheese

4 thick slices iceberg lettuce, for serving

Grated hard-cooked egg, for topping

1. In large bowl, combine extra-virgin olive oil and red wine vinegar with ½ teaspoon each salt and pepper. Stir in plum tomatoes.

2. Stir shredded chicken into dressing, along with avocado, bacon, and blue cheese.

3. Serve over lettuce; top with egg.

SERVES 4: About 425 calories, 27g protein, 12g carbohydrates, 37g fat (9g saturated), 5g fiber, 955mg sodium.

Broccoli-Parmesan Chicken Soup

Silky broccoli soup becomes main dish fare with shredded chicken and a delicious dose of Parmesan.

2 pounds broccoli (about 2 heads)

2 tablespoons olive oil

2 cloves garlic, finely chopped

1 onion, finely chopped

Salt and ground black pepper

½ cup water

4 cups low-sodium chicken broth

3 cups baby spinach

½ cup grated Parmesan

1 tablespoon lemon zest

3 tablespoons lemon juice

2 cups shredded rotisserie chicken

1. Cut tops of broccoli into small florets and thinly slice stems.

2. Heat olive oil in large pot on medium, then add garlic and onion. Cook until sizzling, about 2 minutes. Add broccoli stems, season with ½ teaspoon each salt and pepper, cover, and cook 3 minutes.

3. Add florets and water, cover immediately, and steam until bright green, 3 to 6 minutes. Transfer half of florets to bowl and set aside.

4. Add chicken broth and baby spinach, and simmer 10 minutes. Add Parmesan, lemon zest, and lemon juice, then puree with immersion blender or standard blender. Stir in shredded rotisserie chicken and reserved broccoli florets.

SERVES 4: About 345 calories, 27g protein, 26g carbohydrates, 21.5g fat (5.5g saturated), 8g fiber, 885mg sodium.

TIP

Broccoli's peak season is October through February. Look for firm stalks with tightly closed dark green flowerets when buying produce. To store, place in a breathable plastic bag and place in the refrigerator crisper drawer for up to two days.

Finger-Lickin' Biscuit Loaf

Buffalo chicken and flaky, buttery biscuits team up for this ridiculously tasty pull-apart bread. It's hearty enough to feed a linebacker (or your Sunday Funday crew), no utensils required. #WINNING

PREP: 20 MINUTES   TOTAL: 1 HOUR

6 tablespoons butter, melted

⅓ cup Buffalo-style hot sauce

1½ cup packed finely shredded rotisserie chicken

½ cup crumbled blue cheese

½ cup shredded Cheddar

2 tablespoons snipped chives, plus additional for garnish

1 (16-ounce) tube refrigerated flaky biscuit dough

1. Preheat oven to 350°F. Line 8½ × 4½-inch loaf pan with parchment paper.

2. In medium bowl, combine butter with hot sauce. Add chicken, blue cheese, Cheddar, and chives; toss to coat.

3. Using biscuit dough, separate biscuits into halves and flatten each between your hands. Prop loaf pan up vertically and place 1 biscuit half on bottom. Top with scant 2 tablespoons chicken mixture and another biscuit half. Repeat to form 16 layers.

4. Bake 40 minutes uncovered, then cover with foil and bake 20 minutes more. Cool slightly before serving. Garnish with chives.

SERVES 8: About 358 calories, 16g protein, 26g carbohydrates, 25g fat (12g saturated), 1g fiber, 1,276mg sodium.

Index

Note: Page numbers in *italics* indicate photos separate from recipes.

A

All-natural chicken, 9
Apple & Thyme Roast Chicken, 92
Apples, mini meat loaves with, 106
Arepas, 113
Artichokes
 Chicken with Creamy Spinach, *52–53*
 Skillet Lemon Chicken with Artichokes, *2*, 60
Avocado, chicken sandwiches with, 113

B

Backbone, removing, 12
Bacon. *See* Pancetta and bacon
Bánh mi sandwiches, spicy, 89
Basil & Sun-Dried Tomato Chicken Salad, 117
BBQ Chicken & Cheddar Burgers, *98*, 103
Beans
 Caribbean Chicken & "Rice," *13*, 19
 Paprika Chicken with Tomatoes, *14*, 45
 Sheet Pan Chickpea Chicken, *68–69*
 Skillet Pesto Chicken & Beans, *78–79*
 Slow-Cooker Tex-Mex Soup, 61
Biscuits, bread, and sandwiches
 BBQ Chicken & Cheddar Burgers, *98*, 103
 Buffalo Chicken Baguette Pizza, 112
 Chicken Cutlet Sammies, 50–51
 Chicken Taco Pizzas, *114*–115
 Crispy Chicken Biscuits, *34–35*
 Crispy Hot-Honey Chicken Sliders, 24
 Finger-Lickin' Biscuit Loaf, *122–123*
 Loaded Chicken Burgers, 102
 Pesto Chicken Salad Croissants, 117
 Reina Pepiada, 113
 Spicy Bánh Mi Sandwiches, 89
 Venezuelan Arepas, 113
Bone-in chicken recipes, 59–85
 about: overview of, 59
 Buttermilk Fried Chicken, 65
 Crispy Chicken with White Wine Pan Sauce, *62–63*
 Crunchy Deviled Chicken, *6*, 67
 Fennel Roasted Chicken & Peppers, *76–77*
 Grilled Chicken with White BBQ Sauce, 80
 Honey Mustard–Glazed Chicken Bake, *74–75*
 Moroccan Chicken with Preserved Lemons & Olives, 70
 Mushroom Chicken Skillet with Herbed Cream Sauce, 81
 Nashville Hot Chicken, 64
 Quick Chicken Mole, *58*, 66

Quicker Coq au Vin Blanc, 71
Sheet Pan Chickpea Chicken, *68–69*
Skillet Lemon Chicken with Artichokes, *2*, 60
Skillet Pesto Chicken & Beans, *78–79*
Slow-Cooker Tex-Mex Soup, 61
Spiced Sesame Chicken with Carrots & Couscous, *82–83*
Spicy Jerk Drumsticks, *72–73*
Sweet & Sticky Chicken with Snow Peas, *84–85*
Bourbon BBQ Wings, *100*, 101
Bowls, Provençal chicken quinoa, *16–17*
Breastbone, removing, 12
Breasts, removing skin and nutrition stats, 13
Broccoli
 about: buying tips, 121
 Broccoli-Parmesan Chicken Soup, *120–121*
 Chicken & Broccoli Packets, 40
 Chicken with Roasted Broccoli, *48–49*
Buffalo Chicken Baguette Pizza, 112
Buttermilk Fried Chicken, 65
Buying chicken, 10

C

Cabbage-Kohlrabi Slaw, 97
Caesar (kale), chicken kebabs and, *42–43*
Caribbean Chicken & "Rice," *13*, 19
Carrots, spiced sesame chicken with, *82–83*
Carving tips, 94
Casserole, chicken and broccoli, 41
Cauliflower
 Caribbean Chicken & "Rice," *13*, 19
 Spicy Chicken Miso Stir-Fry, 28
Cheese
 BBQ Chicken & Cheddar Burgers, *98*, 103
 Broccoli-Parmesan Chicken Soup, *120–121*
 Buffalo Chicken Baguette Pizza, 112
 Cheesy Tex-Mex Stuffed Chicken, *30–31*
 Chicken Taco Pizzas, *114*–115
 Feta & Mint Mini Meat Loaves, 107
 Finger-Lickin' Biscuit Loaf, *122–123*
Chicken & Broccoli Casserole, 41
Chicken & Broccoli Packets, 40
Chicken Coconut Curry, 29
Chicken Cutlet Sammies, 50–51
Chicken Kebabs & Kale Caesar, *42–43*
Chicken Marsala Lite, *36–37*
Chicken Roulade with Tomatoes, *54–55*
Chicken with Creamy Spinach, *52–53*
Chicken with Roasted Broccoli, *48–49*
Chicken with Smoky Corn Salad, *20–21*
Chicken/poultry
 all-natural, 9
 buying tips, 10
 cooking with skin, 10

cutting up raw, 12
free-range, 9
fresh, 10
frozen, 10
halal, 10
handling, 10
kosher, 9
nutrition stats, 13
organic, 9
shopping choices, 9–10
storing, 10
thawing, 12
types of, 9
Chickpeas. *See* Beans
Chowder, creamy chicken-corn, *32–33*
Cobb salad, rotisserie chicken, *118–119*
Coconut
 Chicken Coconut Curry, 29
 Coconutty Rice & Peas, 73
Coq au vin blanc, quicker, 71
Corn and polenta
 Chicken with Smoky Corn Salad, *20–21*
 Creamy Chicken-Corn Chowder, *32–33*
 Roasted Chicken & Tomatoes, *46–47*
Cornish hens, *90–91*
Couscous, spiced sesame chicken with carrots and, *82–83*
Creamy Chicken-Corn Chowder, *32–33*
Creamy Lemon Pasta with Chicken, *56–57*
Crispy Chicken Biscuits, *34–35*
Crispy Chicken with White Wine Pan Sauce, *62–63*
Crispy Hot-Honey Chicken Sliders, 24
Crock-Star Chicken with Walnut-Herb Sauce, 97
Croissants, pesto chicken salad, 117
Crunchy Deviled Chicken, *6*, 67
Curry, chicken coconut, 29
Curry-Grape Chicken Salad, 117
Cutting up raw chicken, 12

D

Drumsticks. *See also* Whole-chicken recipes
 about: nutritional stats, 13; removing skin from, 13
 Grilled Chicken with White BBQ Sauce, 80
 Honey Mustard–Glazed Chicken Bake, *74–75*
 Spiced Sesame Chicken with Carrots & Couscous, *82–83*
 Spicy Jerk Drumsticks, *72–73*
 Sweet & Sticky Chicken with Snow Peas, *84–85*

E

Easiest-Ever Paella, *74*, 83
Eggplant
 Grilled Veggies with Honey-Thyme Vinaigrette, *108*, 119

Plum Tomato & Eggplant Shakshuka, *30–31*
Eggs
    Mediterranean Hummus Egg Smash, *12*, 25
    Spanish Potato Omelet, 67
    Summer Squash Frittata, 112
Enchiladas Verdes, *110*, 116

F

Fennel Roasted Chicken & Peppers, *76–77*
Feta & Mint Mini Meat Loaves, 107
Fiery Buffalo Wings, *100*, 101
Fiery Kung Pao Chicken, 25
Finger-Lickin' Biscuit Loaf, *122–123*
Free-range chicken, 9
Freezing poultry, 10
Fresh chicken, buying, 10
Frozen chicken, buying, 10

G

Garlic
    Garlic-Herb Cornish Hens, *90–91*
    Roast Chicken with 40 Cloves of
        Garlic, 93
Green beans, 18, 44, 79
Grilled Chicken with White BBQ Sauce, 80
Ground chicken and meatballs. *See also*
    Meat loaves
        BBQ Chicken & Cheddar Burgers, *98*,
            103
        Lemon-Dill Chicken Meatball Soup,
            108–109
        Loaded Chicken Burgers, 102

        Thai Basil Stir-Fry, *104–105*

H

Halal chicken, 10
Handling and storing poultry, 10
Harissa, ideas for using, 69
Herb Sauce, 91
Honey Mustard–Glazed Chicken Bake,
    74–75
Hot Caribbean Wings, *100*, 101

K

Kale
    Chicken Kebabs & Kale Caesar, *42–43*
    Lighter Chicken Cacciatore, 22
Kebabs, chicken, and kale Caesar, *42–43*
Kosher chicken, 9
Kung pao chicken, fiery, 25

L

Lemon
    Creamy Lemon Pasta with Chicken,
        56–57
    Lemon-Dill Chicken Meatball Soup,
        108–109

Lemon-Pepper Chicken Salad, 117
Lemony Chicken Soup, *38–39*
Lemony Herb Roast Chicken, 96
Moroccan Chicken with Preserved
    Lemons & Olives, 70
Skillet Lemon Chicken with Arti-
    chokes, *2*, 60
Lighter Chicken Cacciatore, 22

Loaded Chicken Burgers, 102

M

Mahogany Roast Chicken, 94
Marsala, chicken (lite), *36–37*
Meat loaves
    about: overview of recipes with wings,
        meatballs and, 99
    Feta & Mint Mini Meat Loaves, 107
    Mustard-Crusted Mini Meat Loaves
        with Roasted Apples, 106
Meatball soup, lemon-dill chicken, *108–109*
Metric conversion charts, 127
Miso, in Spicy Chicken Miso Stir-Fry, 28
Mixed-Nut Spread, 66
Moroccan Chicken with Preserved Lemons
    & Olives, 70
Mushrooms
    Chicken Marsala Lite, *36–37*
    Mushroom Chicken Skillet with Her-
        bed Cream Sauce, 81
Mustard-Crusted Mini Meat Loaves with
    Roasted Apples, 106

N

Nashville Hot Chicken, 64
Nutrition stats, 13
Nuts and seeds
    Crock-Star Chicken with Walnut-Herb
        Sauce, 97
    Mixed-Nut Spread, 66

O

Orange-Ginger Roast Chicken with Fennel
    and Radicchio, *86*, 95
Organic chicken, 9

P

Pancetta and bacon
    Pancetta Chicken, *11*, 18
    Quicker Coq au Vin Blanc, 71
    Rotisserie Chicken Cobb, *118–119*
Paprika Chicken with Tomatoes, *14*, 45
Pasta, creamy lemon with chicken, *56–57*
Peas
    Coconutty Rice & Peas, 73
    Sweet & Sticky Chicken with Snow
        Peas, *84–85*
Peppers, fennel roasted chicken and, *76–77*
Pesto, 79
Pesto Chicken Salad Croissants, 117
Pizzas, 112, *114–115*

Polenta, in Roasted Chicken & Tomatoes,
    46–47
Pomegranate-Glazed Chicken, *13*, 23
Potatoes, dishes with, 71, *74–75*, *90–91*
Prosciutto-Wrapped Chicken, 44
Provençal Chicken Quinoa Bowls, *16–17*

Q

Quick Chicken Mole, *58*, 66
Quicker Coq au Vin Blanc, 71
Quinoa bowls, Provençal chicken, *16–17*

R

Recipes, overview of, 7
Reina Pepiada, 113
Rice
    Caribbean Chicken & "Rice," *13*, 19
    Coconutty Rice & Peas, 73
    Sesame Chicken Stir-Fry, *26–27*
Roast Chicken with 40 Cloves of Garlic, 93
Roasted Chicken & Tomatoes, *46–47*
Roasted Jerk Chicken, *88–89*
Rotisserie chicken meals, *111–123*
    about: overview of, 111
    Broccoli-Parmesan Chicken Soup,
        120–121
    Buffalo Chicken Baguette Pizza, 112
    Chicken Taco Pizzas, *114–115*
    Enchiladas Verdes, *110*, 116
    Finger-Lickin' Biscuit Loaf, *122–123*
    Pesto Chicken Salad Croissants, 117
    Reina Pepiada, 113
    Rotisserie Chicken Cobb, *118–119*

S

Salads
    Basil & Sun-Dried Tomato Chicken
        Salad, 117
    Cabbage-Kohlrabi Slaw, 97
    Chicken Kebabs & Kale Caesar, *42–43*
    Chicken with Smoky Corn Salad, *20–21*
    Curry-Grape Chicken Salad, 117
    Easy Chicken Salad (with variations),
        117
    Lemon-Pepper Chicken Salad, 117
    Rotisserie Chicken Cobb, *118–119*
Sandwiches. *See* Biscuits, bread, and
    sandwiches
Sauces and spreads
    about: fish sauce, 105; making salsa
        verde, 116
    Herb Sauce, 91
    Mixed-Nut Spread, 66
    Pesto, 79
    White BBQ Sauce, 80
    White Wine Pan Sauce, 63
Sesame Chicken Stir-Fry, *26–27*
Sesame Teriyaki Wings, *100*, 101
Sheet Pan Chickpea Chicken, *68–69*

Skillet Lemon Chicken with Artichokes, *2*, 60
Skillet Pesto Chicken & Beans, *78–79*
Skin
    cooking with, benefits, 10
    nutritional impact of removing, 13
    removing, 13
Sliders, crispy hot-honey chicken, 24
Slow-Cooker Tex-Mex Soup, 61
Soups
    Broccoli-Parmesan Chicken Soup, *120–121*
    Creamy Chicken-Corn Chowder, *32–33*
    Lemon-Dill Chicken Meatball Soup, *108–109*
    Lemony Chicken Soup, *38–39*
    Slow-Cooker Tex-Mex Soup, 61
Spiced Sesame Chicken with Carrots & Couscous, *82–83*
Spicy Bánh Mi Sandwiches, 89
Spicy Chicken Miso Stir-Fry, 28
Spicy Jerk Drumsticks, *72–73*
Spinach
    Chicken with Creamy Spinach, *52–53*
    Lemony Chicken Soup, *38–39*
Squash
    Feta & Mint Mini Meat Loaves, 107
    Pomegranate-Glazed Chicken, *13*, 23
    Prosciutto-Wrapped Chicken, 44
Stir-fries
    Sesame Chicken Stir-Fry, *26–27*
    Spicy Chicken Miso Stir-Fry, 28
    Thai Basil Stir-Fry, *104–105*
Storing poultry, 10
Stuffed chicken, cheesy Tex-Mex, *30–31*
Sweet & Sticky Chicken with Snow Peas, *84–85*
Sweet 'n' Sticky Thai Wings, *100*, 10 1

T

Taco pizzas, *114–115*
Tex-Mex soup, slow-cooker, 61
Tex-Mex stuffed chicken, *30–31*
Thai Basil Stir-Fry, *104–105*
Thawing poultry, 12

Thighs. *See also* Whole-chicken recipes
    about: removing skin from, 13
    Crispy Chicken with White Wine Pan Sauce, *62–63*
    Crunchy Deviled Chicken, *6*, 67
    Fiery Kung Pao Chicken, 25
    Grilled Chicken with White BBQ Sauce, 80
    Honey Mustard–Glazed Chicken Bake, *74–75*
    Moroccan Chicken with Preserved Lemons & Olives, 70
    Mushroom Chicken Skillet with Herbed Cream Sauce, 81
    Prosciutto-Wrapped Chicken, 44
    Skillet Lemon Chicken with Artichokes, *2*, 60
    Skillet Pesto Chicken & Beans, *78–79*
    Spiced Sesame Chicken with Carrots & Couscous, *82–83*
    Sweet & Sticky Chicken with Snow Peas, *84–85*
Tomatoes
    Basil & Sun-Dried Tomato Chicken Salad, 117
    Chicken Roulade with Tomatoes, *54–55*
    Paprika Chicken with Tomatoes, *14*, 45
    Roasted Chicken & Tomatoes, *46–47*

V

Venezuelan Arepas, 113

W

Weeknight favorites, *15–57*
    about: overview of, 15
    Caribbean Chicken & "Rice," *13*, 19
    Cheesy Tex-Mex Stuffed Chicken, *30–31*
    Chicken & Broccoli Casserole, 41
    Chicken & Broccoli Packets, 40
    Chicken Coconut Curry, 29
    Chicken Cutlet Sammies, *50–51*
    Chicken Kebabs & Kale Caesar, *42–43*
    Chicken Marsala Lite, *36–37*
    Chicken Roulade with Tomatoes, *54–55*

Chicken with Creamy Spinach, *52–53*
Chicken with Roasted Broccoli, *48–49*
Chicken with Smoky Corn Salad, *20–21*
Creamy Chicken-Corn Chowder, *32–33*
Creamy Lemon Pasta with Chicken, *56–57*
Crispy Chicken Biscuits, *34–35*
Crispy Hot-Honey Chicken Sliders, 24
Fiery Kung Pao Chicken, 25
Lemony Chicken Soup, *38–39*
Lighter Chicken Cacciatore, 22
Pancetta Chicken, *11*, 18
Paprika Chicken with Tomatoes, *14*, 45
Pomegranate-Glazed Chicken, *13*, 23
Prosciutto-Wrapped Chicken, 44
Provençal Chicken Quinoa Bowls, *16–17*
Roasted Chicken & Tomatoes, *46–47*
Sesame Chicken Stir-Fry, *26–27*
Spicy Chicken Miso Stir-Fry, 28
White BBQ Sauce, 80
White wine pan sauce, crispy chicken with, *62–63*
Whole-chicken recipes, *87–97*
    about: carving tips, 94; overview of, 87
    Apple & Thyme Roast Chicken, 92
    Crock-Star Chicken with Walnut-Herb Sauce, 97
    Garlic-Herb Cornish Hens, *90–91*
    Lemony Herb Roast Chicken, 96
    Mahogany Roast Chicken, 94
    Orange-Ginger Roast Chicken with Fennel and Radicchio, *86*, 95
    Roast Chicken with 40 Cloves of Garlic, 93
    Roasted Jerk Chicken, *88–89*
Wings
    about: nutritional stats, 13; overview of recipes with ground chicken and, 99; removing from raw chicken, 12
    Bourbon BBQ Wings, *100*, 101
    Fiery Buffalo Wings, *100*, 101
    Hot Caribbean Wings, *100*, 101
    Sesame Teriyaki Wings, *100*, 101
    Sweet 'n' Sticky Thai Wings, *100*, 101
    Wings of Desire, *100–101*

Photography Credits

Danielle Occhiogrosso Daly: cover, 2, 13, 16, 20, 26, 30, 36, 46, 52, 56, 68, 74, 78, 82, 108, 114, 118, 120, back cover

Mike Garten: 6, 8, 11, 14, 32, 38, 42, 44, 48, 50, 54, 58, 62, 72, 76, 84, 86, 88, 98, 104, 110, 122

© Con Poulos: 34, 90

© Kate Sears: 100

Metric Conversion Charts

The recipes that appear in this cookbook use the standard United States method for measuring liquid and dry or solid ingredients (teaspoons, tablespoons, and cups). The information in these charts is provided to help cooks outside the US successfully use these recipes. All equivalents are approximate.

METRIC EQUIVALENTS FOR DIFFERENT TYPES OF INGREDIENTS

STANDARD CUP	FINE POWDER (e.g., flour)	GRAIN (e.g., rice)	GRANULAR (e.g., sugar)	LIQUID SOLIDS (e.g., butter)	LIQUID (e.g., milk)
¾	105 g	113 g	143 g	150 g	180 ml
⅔	93 g	100 g	125 g	133 g	160 ml
½	70 g	75 g	95 g	100 g	120 ml
⅓	47 g	50 g	63 g	67 g	80 ml
¼	35 g	38 g	48 g	50 g	60 ml
⅛	18 g	19 g	24 g	25 g	30 ml

¼ tsp	=						1 ml
½ tsp	=						2 ml
1 tsp	=						5 ml
3 tsp	=	1 tbsp	=		½ fl oz	=	15 ml
		2 tbsp	=	⅛ cup	=	1 fl oz	=	30 ml
		4 tbsp	=	¼ cup	=	2 fl oz	=	60 ml
		5⅓ tbsp	=	⅓ cup	=	3 fl oz	=	80 ml
		8 tbsp	=	½ cup	=	4 fl oz	=	120 ml
		10⅔ tbsp	=	⅔ cup	=	5 fl oz	=	160 ml
		12 tbsp	=	¾ cup	=	6 fl oz	=	180 ml
		16 tbsp	=	1 cup	=	8 fl oz	=	240 ml
		1 pt	=	2 cups	=	16 fl oz	=	480 ml
		1 qt	=	4 cups	=	32 fl oz	=	960 ml
						33 fl oz	=	1000 ml = 1 L

USEFUL EQUIVALENTS FOR DRY INGREDIENTS BY WEIGHT

(To convert ounces to grams, multiply the number of ounces by 30.)

1 oz	=	¹⁄₁₆ lb	=	30 g
2 oz	=	¼ lb	=	120 g
4 oz	=	½ lb	=	240 g
8 oz	=	¾ lb	=	360 g
16 oz	=	1 lb	=	480 g

USEFUL EQUIVALENTS LENGTH

(To convert inches to centimeters, multiply the number of inches by 2.5.)

1 in	=			2.5 cm
6 in	=	½ ft	=	15 cm
12 in	=	1 ft	=	30 cm
36 in	=	3 ft	=	1 yd	=	90 cm
40 in	=			100 cm = 1 m

USEFUL EQUIVALENTS FOR COOKING/OVEN TEMPERATURES

	Fahrenheit	Celsius	Gas Mark
Freeze Water	32°F	0°C	
Room Temperature	68°F	20°C	
Boil Water	212°F	100°C	
Bake	325°F	160°C	3
	350°F	180°C	4
	375°F	190°C	5
	400°F	200°C	6
	425°F	220°C	7
	450°F	230°C	8
Broil			Grill

TESTED 'TIL PERFECT

Each and every recipe is developed in the Good Housekeeping Test Kitchen, where our team of culinary geniuses create, test, and continue to test recipes until they're perfect. (Even if we make the same dish ten times!)